THE STORY OF

WEST HORSLEY MANOR

AND ITS CHURCH

Pam Bowley

Published by St Mary's Church P.C.C.
West Horsley, Surrey.
1993

Published by St. Mary's Church P.C.C.
West Horsley, Surrey.

By the same author:

The First Thousand Years	1983
The Lovelace Village	1984
The Horsleys in Medieval Times	1985
The Horsleys in World War II	1986
Guide to St. Martin's Church	1986
Woodcote	1988
Guide to St. Mary's Church	1990
Views of Old West Horsley	1991
Inns and Alehouses of Old Horsley	1992

Printed by Rodek Printing Unit 5, Grove Park
Mill Lane, Alton, Hampshire GU34 2QG

CONTENTS

ILLUSTRATIONS

(Drawings and maps by the author, unless otherwise stated)

PREFACE

When one first sets out to write a history of a place, it is a good idea to begin by looking at its name and finding out what its original meaning was. Then one might get a clue about the origins of the village or town in question. So what did Horsley mean? And how did it get its name?

There are at least eight other villages in England with 'Horsley' as their name or as part of their name. It is a Saxon word and the most common translation is "a clearing for horse pasture", but in all living languages the meaning of words gradually change over the centuries, and as the Saxon period in this country stretched over 600 years, it is not surprising if we find that some of the meanings of their words altered, too.

To find out what a name means, it is safest to look at the earliest spelling of that name. But even that is not foolproof, because the actual settlement could be considerably older than that and the name may not have been written down before, so the original meaning could have been forgotten.

The name of this village called Horsley was first mentioned in the Anglo-Saxon Chronicles and is ascribed to a date between AD 871 and 889, during the period when a certain man was Archbishop of Canterbury. The spelling was "Horsalege". But how long the settlement had been in existence before that is something we shall never be able to find out.

Later settlements with names ending in 'ley' usually come from 'leah' meaning a clearing in woodland for pasture. In its turn this word became 'lea' meaning grazing land, such as we see in the name of the Sheepleas. But 'lege' is an older word which meant land or an estate. So "Horsalege" would have meant an "estate belong to Horsa" which was a man's name. In fact the name 'horse' meaning the animal is not a Saxon word, it comes from 'hors' in the old Frisian language and was not in common use until quite late, possibly in the 10th or early 11th century. The early Saxon word for horse was 'pferd', therefore names beginning with Fer or Far may refer to horses. Farley, for instance, is more likely to mean 'a clearing for horse pasture' than Horsley.

But, before we decide finally that this Horsley was founded by a man called Horsa, there is yet another possibility that we could consider – and here we are treading on dangerous ground, for we have no proof of the exact antiquity of this settlement. There is another early word from which the name of Horsley could have derived, and that is 'Hoseli' which meant 'a sacred place where deities were worshipped'. By the Christian period this word came to mean a place where the Eucharist was administered, that is to say, the sanctuary in a church. So when this village was first settled, could 'Hoseli' have referred to a sacred place where, perhaps a water goddess was worshipped, on a little hill from which springs issued forth, and on which a Danish thane later laid down the foundations of St Mary's Church?

3

There is one geographical reason to support this theory, and that is: all the churches and manor houses between Guildford and Leatherhead were built beside the old Iron Age road, with the exception of St Mary's West Horsley, which was built some distance to the south of the old road on a little hill from which two springs emerged, long before the pumping station nearby and the increased demand for water reduced the water table.

P.E.B.

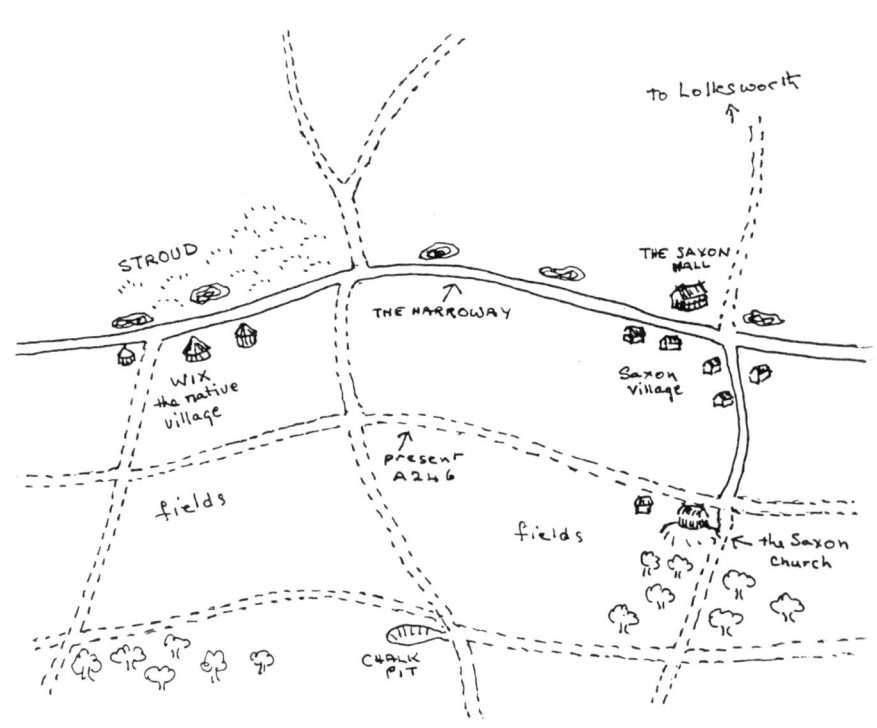

WEST HORSLEY IN SAXON TIMES

▬▬▬▬▬	The Old Iron Age Road known as 'The Harroway'
– – – – –	Other trackways
⬭	Ponds

4

1

THE SAXON AND DANISH PERIOD
AD 410-1066

People have asked me why St Mary's Church is so far away from West Horsley. The answer is that it is the oldest building in the parish and the village has moved away!

The main highways across Surrey in the Neolithic period which ran from Stone Henge to Dover went along the North Downs Way on the chalk downs and the 'Pilgrim's Way,' (a name coined by the Victorians) along the sandstone ridge in the Weald. At that time most of England was covered in dense woodland and only the tops of the hills were cultivated where the soil was too shallow for many trees to grow.

By the Iron Age, however, when iron axes enabled the dense woodland on the sides of the hills to be cleared, a new route on the dip-slope of the North Downs became the main highway. This ran along the spring-line at the foot of the downs on a narrow bed of Thanet sand between the chalk and the clay. It was known as 'The Harroway' from 'hoar weg' meaning 'the old way'.

The Harroway was in use before the Romans came, and later when the Saxons arrived in our part of Surrey, they made their settlements beside it. At West Horsley there was already a Romano-British village roughly where Wix Farm is, and the Saxons made their settlement in the vicinity of West Horsley Place. This fact suggests that the Saxons lived peacefully beside the original inhabitants in this area.

Between the ford at Leatherhead and the ford at Guildford, Saxon settlements grew up at Fetcham, Bookham, Effingham, Dirtham, Horsley and Clandon. The Thane's halls and the churches were all built on either side of this old road. West Horsley was the exception. Here, although the thane's hall and his people's huts were beside the old road, the church was built at a short distance away on a small hill.

Christianity first came to England in the 2nd century AD during the Romano-British period, but after the Romans left in 410 AD, Christianity began to decline. When the Saxons invaded England they were pagans, worshipping many deities.

St Augustine landed in Kent in the year 597 AD and set up a mission to convert the heathen Saxons. He started by converting the King and the noblemen, who in their turn commanded all their subordinates to follow suit. But many of them continued worshipping their old gods whilst also giving lip service to Christianity. Therefore, Augustine urged that churches should be set up in the pagan places of worship, so people could only worship in one place. But before churches were built, itinerant monks travelled the country-side from the nearest religious houses setting up portable altars and preaching to the people.

St Mary's Church stands on a little hill below which two springs emerged. These now rise further north of West Horsley Place, because the water table has fallen. It is quite possible that a shrine to a water goddess or a fertility goddess stood on the hill above the springs as sources of springs were considered to be "holy" places and that is, perhaps, why the church was built there, and dedicated to St Mary.

The earliest mention of the name Horsley, was in the Anglo-Saxon Chronicles. It was in the will of a Saxon Duke called Elfrede and has been dated to between 871 and 899 AD. Beside Horsley, Elfrede owned many other estates in both Surrey and Kent. Places like Clapham (which was once in Surrey), Sanderstead, Selsdon, Lingfield, Gatton, Westerham and several others which cannot be identified with modern names.

In his will Elfrede's sons inherited his various estates but "Horsalege" was left to his wife Werburgh for life, and after that to his daughter Aldryth and her future children. But the interesting thing is that in his will he also left "twa wergeld" to "Sancte Petre" which would be St Peter's Abbey at Chertsey. Other words used in the will are "Godes willa", "God almahtig" and the name "Cristes" is repeated several times. So this proves that Elfrede was a Christian,

How the first Saxon church may have looked

therefore, there may have been a church in Horsley as early as the 9th century. If that was the case, it was probably built of split tree trunks like the one at Ongar in Essex.

About the time that Elfrede's will was drawn up, Surrey was already being over-run by Danish war-parties whose speciality was looting and burning churches. This continued until 1016 when the Danish King Canute, became king of England.

When the chalk clunch foundations of our present church were laid, it is believed in about 1030, Horsley was owned by a *Danish* thane. It may have been the same man, called Thored, who gave a strip of his land to the Archbishop of Canterbury six years later "for the good of his soul". This piece of land, together with another landholding known as "Horsley Episcopi", became the present East Horsley.

The Formation of English Parishes

Most of our existing parishes today have their origins in Saxon times. The Saxon community was initially organised into groups of homesteads who cultivated fields which they held in common, and who served a local lord. The community had to be large enough to supply 10 able bodied men to serve with his lord when occasions required a fighting force. These groups were known as 'tithings' and in turn they were grouped together in 'hundreds'. West Horsley belonged to the Woking Hundred which was very much larger in area than the Effingham Hundred, thus showing that the population of the Woking Hundred was much sparser than that of Effingham.

As the Church advanced its missionary work, the first little wooden churches were built by local lords or thanes. They claimed the right of appointing the parish priest, a right which has come down in some parishes until the present day. The nearness of the manor house to the church in so many villages bears witness to this close relationship. In the early days, the parish priests were chaplains to Saxon thanes, they were not monks and they were often married. The priest's duty required him to celebrate seven services daily, but after the eleventh century these were reduced to three daily services.

Each lord's church came under the supervision of a nearby monastery or ecclesiastic college – West Horsley came under Chertsey Abbey – and eventually each manor's territorial unit made up a legal and administrative unit. Where the population was sparse, one parish would contain, and still often does, more than one village and more than one lord's holding. The two small sub-manors of Wix and Lollesworth came under West Horsley's parish church.

2

THE SAXON CHURCH

Possible appearance of the chalk and flint Saxon Church with an apsidal chancel end.

At the time of the Norman Conquest in 1066, the Saxon Church which stood here was the same length and width as the present nave which is built on the foundations of the Saxon church. The walls were constructed of blocks of chalk clunch, (a hard solidified form of chalk) quarried no doubt from the ancient chalk pit beside Shere Road.

There were no side aisles and there was apparently no tower. At the east end there may have been a semicircular or squarish sanctuary, and probably a tall slim archway between the sanctuary and the nave. Another possibility may have been a rarer feature, namely a triple chancel arch, with the central one being higher than the two outer ones. This sometimes appeared in later Saxon churches and the remains of the small arch seen today at the left of the present chancel arch may be part of this triple arch feature. After measuring the half-arch that remains and the full length of the east wall, one will see that there is ample room for three arches of the same width with a narrow pillar in between.

The only other explanation for the remaining half of this archway is that there was originally a narrow central arch, which was more common, and that in the Medieval period a 'squint' was cut into the wall so that the congregation could get a glimpse of the priest at the altar. Later this squint could have been made into a doorway with a staircase behind it for the musicians to climb up onto the Rood Screen.

Probably the only entrance to the church would have been at the west end where the present door to the tower is. There would have

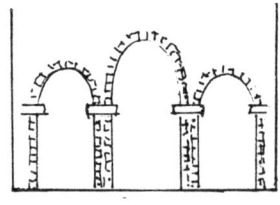

A triple Saxon Arch

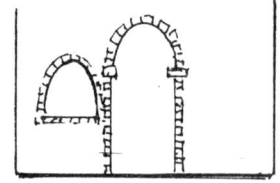

A Saxon Arch with Medieval Squint

8

been a steep thatched roof and small unglazed slit windows high up in the two side walls to let in the light. The reason for them being so high up may have been to eliminate the draught. The floor would have been of beaten earth and chalk, strewn with rushes. This original floor still exists beneath the pew-platforms of the nave. The walls most likely were covered with a plaster made of lime, cow-dung, and hair.

At the time of the Battle of Hastings, West Horsley belonged to a Danish thane called Beorhtsige or Brictsi, as it is more commonly spelt. His main landholding was in Kent and he was an important and influential man and was married to one of King Harold's sisters. His Surrey estates included Compton, near Guildford, Stoke D'Abernon and Brixton (now in London, but once in Surrey) which took its name from him. It is more than likely that Brictsi was close beside King Harold during the fatal battle at Hastings and died with him on the battlefield.

Elated with their victory, William the Conqueror and his men travelled throughout the south-east region burning and looting all the villages belonging to thanes who had fought with King Harold and who did not submit to him afterwards. West Horsley was one of these villages which was razed to the ground.

Like all the other Danish and Saxon thanes, Brictsi had his estates confiscated and given to relatives and friends of the new king, William. A man called Walter Fitz Otha received West Horsley and Compton, and shortly afterwards he was made governor of Windsor Castle and took the surname "de Windsor".

When we talk about the village of West Horsley in those days we should remember that it would have been extremely small, consisting of the thane's hall and a few huts around it. The total population may not have exceeded about 200, and some of these would have been in scattered farms around the area. After the village was burnt down it went into a decline. It is probable that many of the able bodied men had been killed at Hastings fighting in their lord's service.

The de Windsor family's principal seat was at Stanwell in Essex, but beside Compton and West Horsley, they also owned other estates in Surrey, such as Peperharow and Hurtmore. There is evidence that they lived at Compton for part of the time as they had a house there and it looks as though they may not have had a residence at Horsley, except perhaps a timber-framed hall where the lord of the manor or his representative could spend the night when presiding over the Manorial Courts Baron or Leet.

Between the years 1080 to 1185, the de Windsor family transformed the Saxon church at Compton into a very lavishly styled Norman one, for although the Normans were known to be cruel and harsh masters, they grudged no money when it came to building and beautifying churches. But St Mary's remained as a rustic church and little or nothing was done to it.

The first addition to the church that we know of was the tower built of chalk and flint in about 1120, It was built up against the wall of the church and not bonded in. This was when the de Windsors were still resident at Compton. So could it be that the people of the parish decided to build the tower themselves and not the lord of the manor? These were unsettled times in our island history. The first holy war of the Crusades had just finished and we were under threat of invasion by Robert the Norman. Folk memory may well have included the previous coming of the Normans and the burning and pillaging of the village. The people probably felt vulnerable without a resident lord to protect them. The church would have been the only building in the village with solid walls, all other buildings would have been constructed of timber and wattle.

At this time church towers were not used solely as belfries, though they did often contain a bell for warning the people of trouble or the start of Services. Their most important role may have been a defensive one – they were useful as look-out posts, places of refuge and a depository for church valuables and communal village property such as seed corn and defensive weapons. Sometimes, there was also a room up in the tower in which a priest lived.

In our church tower there were originally two rooms, one above the other, and it is interesting to note that the ladder in the tower must date from when the tower was first built, because it is made of a single tall tree which has been split in half and there is no way it could have been brought into the tower at a later date because of its length. There would not have been a spire at first, only a small gabled or pyramid shaped thatched roof.

The original entrance door into the tower and the church was probably a plain Norman arch, but flint is not an easy building material and needs the use of something more solid for corners or doors and windows, and here, the only "stone" was chalk clunch which is fairly soft. This doorway must have required repairing many times, and one interesting thing that I noticed about it is that on the right-hand side there is a deep hole and above it, a little to the inside of the door jamb are signs of smoke staining. This must have been the hole in which a large iron ring or hook protruded on which was supported either a flaming torch or a lantern to light the congregation into church when it was dark.

3

THE DE WINDSOR FAMILY
1066-1271

The descendants of Walter Fitz Otha continued to hold the office of Governor of Windsor Castle and retained the surname 'de Windsor'. But between 1160 and 1194, we find that a "Sir Hugh de Horslegh (alias de Windsor)" held a knight's fee at Horsley and gave a large part of the tithes of his lordship in Horsley to the Abbey of Chertsey. He was a grandson or great grandson of Walter Fitz Otha and perhaps a younger son of his father. [A knight's fee was a variable measure of land considered to be sufficient to support a knight and his family for a year.]

It is logical to presume that Hugh de Windsor built himself a new manor house at Horsley when he came to live here, and it may have been that the manor was a wedding gift from his father. There is evidence that this first house was a moated manor house, which was fashionable at the time. The moat also served the purpose of draining the ground around the site which could have been a necessary factor here as the house was close to the spring line.

It is also possible that this was the time when the deer park was created around the manor house and any inhabitants still living on the site of the earlier village were moved away towards 'Stroud', which was the old settlement that lay near the boundary with East Clandon, and was part of a sub-manor called Weke [Wix Farm]. Another name for it may have been Strudwick, (Stroud wick) as part of the common field bore that name.

The Compton manor was undoubtedly held by the main line of the de Windsor family, but by about 1185 they had set about dividing it up into several portions of land and began leasing it out to various sub-feudatory lords, until finally in 1196, Walter de Windsor sold the lease of the last half of a knight's fee to Hugh de Polstead and his wife Cecily.

Once Hugh de Horslegh (or de Windsor) and his family had established a household at West Horsley they turned their attention to St Mary's church. By this time a plainer style of architecture was coming in called 'Early English'. In about 1190, Hugh de Windsor demolished the north wall of the church and constructed a narrow north aisle which was about half the width of the present one. The original wall was replaced by an arcade of four pointed arches supported by three circular columns, surmounted by circular capitals. A new entrance in the centre of this aisle was constructed facing the manor house. This was presumably for the convenience of the family, so they did not have to enter by the same door as the peasants.

The new aisle may have contained a family pew because the north wall of the new aisle had two windows with pointed heads to the east of the new entrance door.

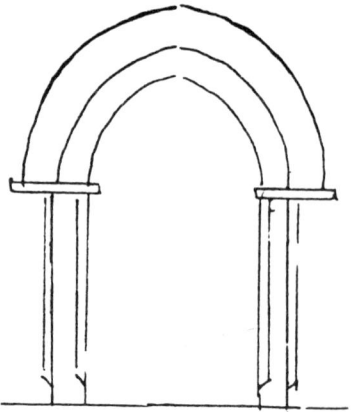

The West Door

They may have been put there expressly for the purpose of providing light in this family pew, for apart from some small lancets in the chancel, these were still the only windows of any size in the church. If there was a family pew here, that may have been a reason for creating a 'squint' through to the chancel.

The new north door was built in a simple Early English style with a slightly pointed arch and jambs of three concentric arches. The present north doorway is the original one which was moved forward when the aisle was widened in 1849. This doorway still shows some original tooling marks

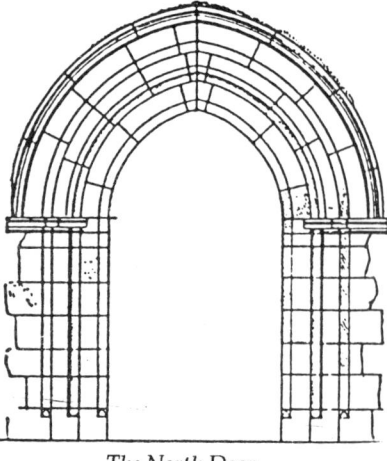

The North Door

and some incised pilgrims' or consecration crosses on the jambs.

When this work had been completed, the west door from the nave into the tower, which may have been only a plain arch before that, was embellished on the outside in a similar way, but with jambs of only two concentric arches. This suggests that it was still used as a main entrance to the church by the ordinary parishioners.

In 1194 Sir Hugh and his son Walter, went to Normandy in the service of King Richard I. Hugh must have died there because we find in the following year, the lord of the manor was a Sir Walter de Windsor; but it wasn't for long, because in 1197 there was a second Sir Hugh who may have been Sir Walter's younger brother.

This Sir Hugh, we will call him "the second Sir Hugh" for convenience sake, may not have been married, for he had no direct heirs. He divided the income

12

of the manor of West Horsley between himself and another of his brothers called William, who also died shortly afterwards in Normandy. Reading between the lines, it seems possible that the second Sir Hugh may have been the parish priest as well as the lord of the manor. When he died in 1220, he was succeeded by his brother William's son, a third Sir Hugh.

The Second Sir Hugh de Windsor 1197-1220

The 2nd Sir Hugh de Windsor spent a lot of his time and money on improving the church. A major task he undertook was to build a new chancel in about 1210. The chancel arch was probably enlarged at this time too, but it may not have been as high or wide as the present one and there is a good reason to believe that the present chancel arch was enlarged at a later date again. The left-hand Saxon arch may have been retained complete and the new arch took over most of the space of the other two arches to the side. [The present chancel arch is not in the centre of this wall either!]

As the church might have been in 1066

Soon after the chancel was completed, a huge rood-screen was erected across the east wall of the nave with a rood-loft over it where the musicians would sit to play their instruments. Legend has it that they entered by the small arch below, climbed a spiral staircase, in the corner of the chancel, and came out on to the loft above through the wooden frame which remains in the wall today. This is only a crude frame because it would not have been visible to the congregation. Above the rood-loft hung a huge rood (holy cross with Christ crucified upon it) which was suspended from a large beam, the sawn-off ends of which can still be seen above the chancel arch.

Some alterations seem to have been made to the north wall of the chancel since it was built because it is thinner than the east and south walls, and the whole wall seems to have been moved inwards by about two feet. There is a stone coffin [could it be that of the 2nd Sir Hugh who built the chancel?] embedded into the wall instead of lying in front of it, and the north wall ends up behind the blocked half-archway that remains today. This wall must have been altered at a much later date in an effort to centralise the chancel arch a little more – at the beginning of the 19th century perhaps

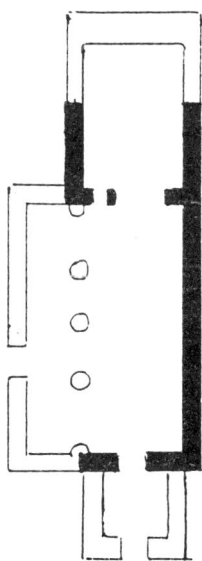

As it might have looked in 1250

13

when a vestry room was built outside in the angle of the chancel and north aisle.

There is a marked twist in the axis of the chancel towards the north. It is what is called a "weeping chancel" and is found in many old churches. Tradition has it that it was intended to symbolise the droop of Our Lord's head as He hung on the cross. But of course it may have been unintentional as medieval workmen did not have the instruments to help them such as a builder would use today. Tradition also has it that the central window of the east wall of the chancel faces the point where the sun rises on the saint's day to which the church is dedicated.

The St Catherine roundel

The chancel is unusually long in shape and allowed plenty of room for the ritual of the early English church. It may be that it was intended to make ample room for the family tombs and memorials of the Patrons of the Church. At the east end there are three tall lancet windows with detached shafts with moulded bases and capitals.

Until the 13th century, windows had been very small as glass was expensive and hard to come by. However, the windows in the chancel must have been glazed from the start. There is one original roundel and a medallion both dated about 1210. The roundel in the north light portrays the martyrdom of St Catherine and the medallion in the centre is of Mary Magdalene anointing the feet of Jesus. There is a similar roundel in Compton church of the same date and they are the oldest surviving fragments of stained glass in Surrey, and were no doubt, gifts from the de Windsor family. The third medallion showing the Annunciation of the Blessed Virgin Mary was made around 1900 especially to balance up the windows.

The bowl of the font dates from about 1200 and was originally plain hewn sandstone, but the tooling was done on the outside in the last century. It bears signs that the original font cover had hinges and fastenings. Before the Reformation, Holy Water was thought to have magical properties, therefore the font was kept locked.

Another gift to the church in about 1220 was the old Parish Chest. It is purported to be one of seven chests distributed throughout the country and is believed to be the work of a John de Leighton. The chest is bound with iron straps and at either end are the remains of drop-handles.

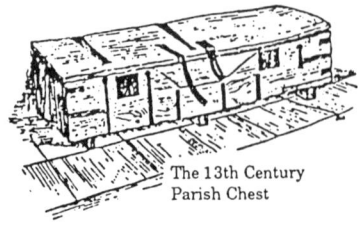

The 13th Century Parish Chest

Church chests were important pieces of furniture, for in them were kept the priest's vestments, church plate, service books, money and any holy relics that the church might own. Later, they housed parish registers and parishioners' wills. At one time there would have been three locks with different keys – one kept by the priest and the others by the two Church Wardens. The chest could only be opened when all three were present.

The Wall Paintings

It may also have been the second Sir Hugh de Windsor who was responsible for the wall paintings in our church. They are believed to date from about 1200, and were discovered and expertly investigated in 1970 and finally restored with great care two years later.

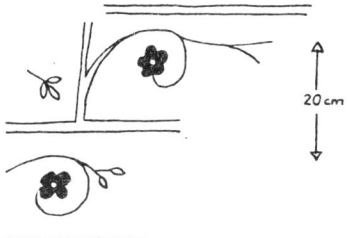

Sketch of the masonry pattern found on the south wall in 1970

It was clear from the investigation that in the 13th century the whole of the interior walls, and the north arcade with its pillars had been painted with pictures and designs. Those in the chancel, the earlier north aisle and the north arcade had been destroyed during the renovations which took place in 1849, but from the remaining medieval plaster in the church, it was possible to piece together some evidence of the medieval décor.

Upon the whole of the east wall of the Nave and around the corner above part of the south arcade there were masonry patterns with roses and leaves drawn in red ochre. There were traces of a stripe design around part of the chancel arch and traces of a chevron design on one of the pillars. On the right-hand side of the west wall of the Nave stands a 13ft high figure of St Christopher, full faced and bearing the Christ-Child upon his left shoulder. His right hand is lost but it certainly once held the top of his staff which continues down the side of the painting with a line of roses beside it. The legend was that after he carried Christ across the river, his staff sprouted flowers and leaves. The latter were probably painted in green, a fugitive colour that has now disappeared.

On the left-hand side of the west wall is a fragment of the Passion Cycle measuring $8^1/2 \times 5$ feet. This subject once continued around the south west corner and along the original south wall. The

15

painting is a strip-story in three tiers with a decorative dado-band between each. The scenes run on without any vertical divisions between, but the division is made by the figures standing back to back. In the upper tier there is the Crucifixion with Longinus and one thief. In the middle tier are the Scourging and Christ carrying the Cross. The lower tier shows the Risen Christ handing St Peter the keys of heaven, and the devil gloating over the wicked souls in the flames of hell. Around the corner on part of the old south wall are some roses and part of an angel. This may have been the scene of Christ's Resurrection or perhaps the Annunciation. There is also a pattern both here and between the lines of paintings on the west wall which looks like fishes swimming along, or it might be a tendril design.

The pigments used for painting were of the simplest kind, oxides of iron being the commonest – red and yellow ochre which could be varied and mixed into a wide range of colours from purple to pale red. Lime white and lamp black or charcoal were also common and could be mixed with other pigments to vary the tones. Greens were generally a copper salt but were not as permanent as the red oxides and have mostly faded by now. Blue was rare and expensive.

Naturally the great cathedrals would have had access to the best artists, but there were many competent artists available for the humbler churches who were, no doubt, commissioned for this work by a wealthy Lord of the Manor.

There are many churches in Surrey with paintings of St Christopher on their walls. He was the patron saint of travellers, and in medieval days one was in dire need of protection, not only from the bands of cut-throats and robbers who roamed the countryside but also the wolves in the forest. It was generally believed if you looked upon a picture of St Christopher each day of your journey you would be safe from danger.

The prime object of the wall paintings was not merely to beautify the house of God, though that was probably true to a certain extent, but to teach the illiterate population about the scriptures. The few books that existed at the time were generally written in Latin or Norman French and only a very small percentage of people could read them. Usually the only scholars were clerics and quite often even the Lord of the Manor could not read, so he would employ a cleric to do all his written work for him. This being the case, the strip stories and pictures of the saints were very important and could be described as the Poor Man's Bible, the priest using them as a "visual aid" for his teaching.

Village congregations needed help in recognising the characters portrayed, so an elaborate code of symbolism was employed in these paintings. Good people had haloes and were beautifully drawn, while bad people were made ugly with hooked noses and hump backs. Also the type of headgear or the way a hand was held or legs placed told the beholder who or what the characters were, and each saint had his or her own special emblem.

To the average medieval peasant living in his hovel, who had seldom travelled more than a few miles from the place where he was born, the village church must have been a wondrous place. The Sunday High Mass was the centre of worship: at this, the incumbent, supported by an assistant priest or chantry chaplain, both wearing rich robes, chanted the service at the High Altar. The Chancel would be brightly lit by candles and oil lamps and the congregation, either standing or kneeling on the earth floor of the less well-lit and unfurnished Nave, would behold the spectacle through the traceried Rood-screen. The vision of the brighter world beyond must have been very impressive after the squalid, smokey huts in which they lived.

The Third Sir Hugh de Windsor

The second Sir Hugh de Windsor died in about 1220, and as I said before, it is possible that the stone coffin embedded in the wall near the altar may contain his remains, because it was he who rebuilt the chancel and did so much to make the church more beautiful. His nephew, the third Sir Hugh inherited the Manor, but

St Mary's Church as it may have looked in about the year 1200

whereas his uncle comes over as a saintly old bachelor, doing much to improve the church, the third Sir Hugh, sounds like a more worldly character. He spent most of his time putting the estate to rights and exacting the dues from the tenants, but may not have done much for the church.

There are several things we know about the third Sir Hugh from the Court Rolls, the Surrey Eyres and other sources, for he seemed to spend much of his time in litigation against lease holders in Compton, his landed neighbours and his tenants in West Horsley and other manors he held. Perhaps his uncle had let the estate matters get a little lax, for in his efforts to make sure the peasants did their obligatory numbers of "boon days" on his land – that means the number of days they had to work in lieu of rent – the third Sir Hugh stirred up a hornets nest!

In 1232 a certain Hamo de la Wudecote, who some years earlier he had forced to exchange half a hide of land with him, now brought him to court for demanding services from him, for he claimed that he was a "free man". Freemen were jealous of their rights and resisted any attempt to encroach on them. Other less fortunate villagers, the villeins and bondmen, had to work for a certain number of days in the month or year for the lord of the manor as an obligation of their tenancy.

In the 13th century the population was increasing rapidly and the land was being used intensively, but at subsistence level. Waste land was coming under cultivation and the price of pasture land was becoming too high for most peasants. The poor sold off what remained of their heritage – their strips in the common fields and their pasture rights – to the more affluent villagers and landowners who then built up their stakes in the land.

In 1242, Sir Hugh de Windsor bought up the rights of common pasture on 80 acres of land in West Horsley. This may have been Barnsthorns Woods which at that time was common land lying within the parish, used as pasture for pigs. He may have fenced it in and made it into another deer park, because later he was "granted free warren in his **two** parks at West Horsley" by Henry III. The other park would have been that already existing around the Manor House. "Free Warren" meant he had the right to hunt game animals and game birds over the whole area of his land holding, including any land held by tenants. He also had the right to have a rabbit warren on his land. Rabbits were introduced into England by the Normans and it was a privilege held by certain members of the nobility to own a warren, which was either a natural or artificial mound with a fence around it. There was one behind Place Farm. Any peasant who killed an escaped rabbit, even if it was eating his crops, was severely punished.

In the following century, this land which Sir Hugh had bought from the peasants became known as "Berner's Thorn Wood", it is now called "Barnsthorns Woods" and the land adjacent to it in East Horsley which is now called "The Forest" was formerly called "Thornleys". Each parish had its own area for growing thorn trees (hawthorn and blackthorn) because thorn trees played an important part in medieval husbandry. They were used to make "dead hedges" around the crops to protect them from animals and to keep their stock confined to other areas where they were supposed to be grazing.

In 1255 Sir Hugh held the wardship of Richard de Wykes of the sub-manor of Wykes (or Wekes or Wix), and he had an action brought against him by the parson of West Horsley, Richard de Windsor, who may have been a younger brother or an uncle. Then in 1258 he married a wealthy widow called Godeholda de Ros, who brought with her an inheritance which included land in Essex, Kent and Tatsfield, Surrey. This was probably a second marriage for he must have been quite advanced in years by this time.

In 1264 it looks as though he had backed the wrong side during the Barons' War because he had to pay a heavy fine and the manor of West Horsley was assessed as being worth £19 10s. 4d.

4

THE DE BERNERS FAMILY
1271-1441

The third Sir Hugh must have been well into his seventies when he died, a remarkable achievement in those days. His death occurred sometime before 1271, because in that year we find his executors litigating about the wardship of Henry, son of Richard de Wykes. His son, the fourth Sir Hugh de Windsor set about giving away the family's very considerable land holdings which included estates and rents in Chiddingfold, Cranleigh, Send, Shere, Wisley, Effingham, East Horsley, Ockham and Ockley.

de Berners
1271 - 1441

The major recipient was Sir Ralph de Berners of Berners Roding in Essex, the husband of his daughter, Christiana de Windsor. In return for this gift Sir Ralph had to pay £10 annual rent during Hugh's lifetime and after that for $^1/_2$lb of cumin-seed to Hugh's heirs (worth about 1d.) Although £10 was a lot of money in those days, the endowment was nevertheless a generous one, because it also included land in Effingham, Ockham, Send and Wisley. Sir Ralph also acquired the right to "free warren" and the right to be free from toll at Guildford because his manor was held of the Barony of Windsor.

In 1279 doubts had arisen about the sanity of the fourth Sir Hugh de Windsor and the matter was referred to Parliament. The result was that the new owners kept the lands they had been given and Sir Hugh was made a King's ward as an idiot.

By this time, St Mary's Church was already nearly 300 years old and the roof of the Nave was said to be in a rotten state and required rebuilding. So somewhere between 1270 and 1300, the de Berners had a major job on their hands. The line of the roof was raised slightly when the new timbers were put in place, and the tie-beams inserted at this time are still there today. The line of the old roof can still be seen over the west wall of the nave, and instead of thatch, the new roof was now covered with Horsham slab – a kind of thick slate.

Christiana de Berners' husband died in 1297 and she took over the estate in her own right as Lady of the Manor. Her eldest son, Edmund, who was the heir to the estate went away to Normandy and seems to have died there in about 1316 leaving as his heir an infant son called John.

19

While Christiana was administering the estate she became involved with major wrangles concerning two of her sons. The first was in 1309 when she presented Roger de Berners, possibly her third son, as Rector. The king disputed her right of advowson as the rightful heir was a minor, and wished to appoint John de Ockham, who later became the great lawyer-priest at Oxford. However, the courts decided in favour of Christiana and her son Roger was duly installed, but this proved to be a disaster.

Roger turned out to be a waster and bent on pleasure. He did not take his duties seriously, and in 1317 it was recorded that he had allowed the chancel, the church books and ornaments, the parsonage and the woods belonging to it, all to fall into a state of neglect. (This early parsonage house probably stood on the site of Church House). The Bishop of Winchester ordered the stipend, tithes and other income due to the incumbent to be taken away. Shortly afterwards he was accused of having married and therefore broken the Church's rule of celibacy for priests. He was finally removed from the living in 1317 and took up residence in East Horsley where he became involved in several dubious land dealings.

The other dispute which Christiana became involved in was with her second son, Richard who claimed certain free tenements and land in West Horsley. It might have been that because his elder brother was dead he thought he should be the heir to the estate instead of the infant John. The matter seemed to be resolved temporily, but after his mother's death, it came up again in 1325. John was still a minor and the estate was being administered by John Waleweyn (possibly the Land Steward) and the Rector, Stephen le Blound. A petition was sent to Parliament, but Richard lost his suit and later, in 1337, his son Thomas made it known that he "relinquished all rights to the manor and advowson of West Horsley".

The only thing we know of the first John de Berners is that after he had reached his majority, he obtained a licence from the Bishop to have a chapel in his manor house at West Horsley. Perhaps he was in ill health and couldn't manage the walk to the church, for he died quite young in 1341. But before his death he had obviously married for he was succeeded by his infant son, another John.

This second John also died young and left an infant son called James, but not before he had appointed four trustees to administer the manors of West Horsley and Berners Roding in Essex. These included Thomas de Weston, Lord of the Manor of Albury and Richard Hertewell, the Rector of West Horsley. They were instructed to secure the succession of James to his inheritance and also to provide for a relative, Ralph de Berners, a clerk in Holy Orders, who was to receive a pension of £10 a year from the rents of the manors – this was a considerable sum in those days. The family must have been fond of him and indebted to him for some reason – perhaps he had been guardian to one or both of the infant John de Berners.

20

The Black Death – 1349

There were many natural disasters in the first half of the 14th century which caused widespread starvation among the poorer people. There were recurring outbreaks of disease among cattle and sheep and a long series of droughts, floods, storms and cold wet summers which created bad harvests. Finally, when the Black Death arrived in 1349, the people had little

The Old Red Lion Inn

resistance. It is estimated that the population of England was nearly halved, and one can only assume that this parish did not get off lightly, as there is a general lack of information about this period.

Although we have dates for two Rectors – 1329 John Palmer de Bisshopeston and 1357 Richard Palmer, we do not know if John Palmer survived the Black Death. The clergy, especially those in Religious Houses, were among those who suffered badly, probably because of their obligation for hospitality towards travellers and their duty to care for the sick. After the ravages of the plague, it is said that there was a long period when it was difficult to find anyone who could read and write; therefore, when a parish did find a new priest, he was often illiterate and badly trained. It is quite possible that West Horsley was without a permanent priest for about eight years until Richard Palmer was instituted.

With the horror of the Black Death still in their minds, the Patron and parishioners may have decided to move their future priests' dwelling to a safer place further away from the main road and to build an inn beside the church. Sometime between the Black Death and 1400 a new parsonage was built beside the old village green with a tithe barn and farm buildings, together with new glebe lands. An inn called "The Red Lion" was built beside the church to accommodate pilgrims and travellers. This building is still standing and is now a private house called "Church House", and the old tithe barn still remains behind the "Old Rectory".

Sir James de Berners 1348-1388

The second Sir John de Berners did not live at West Horsley, for he had appointed four men to look after the estate. Perhaps he was away fighting in France. When he died in 1362, his son James was only 14 years old and did not inherit the estate until he came of age.

As often happened with young noblemen, Sir James de Berners was

21

Portrait of Sir James de Berners in the north window of the chancel

brought up at court. He became a great favourite of the young King Richard II, and therefore stirred up jealousy among the other nobles, who blamed him for the king's misrule. In 1388 he was arrested, beheaded on Tower Hill and his estates confiscated. Although the king was unable to save him, five years later he was able to restore the Manor of West Horsley with the park and warrens to Sir James' widow, the Lady Anne.

Although Sir James must have been absent from the parish for most of the period he was Lord of the Manor, several embellishments to the chancel were placed there in his time which are still with us today.

In about 1370 a fine reredos made of brightly painted and carved alabaster was placed behind the altar. When it was complete it may have depicted the life of Christ, but there only remains one fragment of it representing the Nativity. This was found in 1810 beneath the old brick floor when a new flagstone floor was laid. It shows the Virgin Mary, crowned with a halo, looking at the Holy Baby lying in an oval cradle. In the background is the figure of an angel, the head of Joseph with long hair and beard, and the heads of the ox and ass. The carving is very fine and there are still traces of red, black and gold paint in the crevices.

In the north wall of the chancel is a recessed tomb made of chalk clunch with a life-size effigy of a priest robed in Mass

The tomb of a priest in the chancel

22

vestments. It is the earliest carved representation of a priest in Surrey and is believed to be Ralph de Berners, the kinsman who may have been guardian and confidant to the two John de Berners and possibly James as well, who were all underage when they inherited the manor. He lies with his hands joined in prayer and has little angels, known as "weepers" at his feet. The tomb recess is canopied under an ogee arch with ornamentation which includes monkeys' heads – an emblem of the de Berners' family.

Over the tomb is a handsome cinque-foil window, almost identical to two in the nave of Ockham Church which may have been made by the same masons. In this window is a glazed portrait of Sir James de Berners in the centre light. He is bearded and is kneeling with hands together in prayer. He wears chain mail, over which is a tabard bearing the de Berners arms and a sword hangs from his side. The white glass used for the figure has a greenish hue and most likely came from Chiddingfold, one of the few glass-making centres in England at the time, and the design is painted on and then burned in. It was made before Sir James' death in 1388, and is believed to be only part of the original painted glass which had originally filled the triple-light window. This panel was chosen to be exhibited at the "Age of Chivalry" exhibition at the Royal Academy in London in 1987/88.

Other work that was carried out on the church during the time of Sir James de Berners in about 1370, was the placing of a spire on top of the tower, which was the same shape as it is today, and the replacing of the original outside doorway into the tower with a new one with a pointed, moulded arch. The original Norman arch was likely to have been of chalk clunch which is very soft and would have weathered badly. Two new wooden doors were put in at the same time. The one in the West door of the tower with plain strap hinges may be the original, but the one in the North door is a Victorian replica which was made when the north aisle was widened.

The west porch was built in 1380 and much of the original work remains. It is of timber framing resting on low flint walls, much of which has been replaced with brick. The present open sides were originally enclosed with either wattle and daub or, possibly, pierced tracery carved in wood. There is a king post and a fine cusped barge-board, similar in design to the barge boards on the south side of West Horsley Place and at Lower Hammonds Farm on Ripley Lane. They are all about the same date.

As well as protecting the entrance door from the weather, the church porch had many uses in medieval times. Baptisms and wedding ceremonies started in the porch and public notices were posted there. It was a local meeting place for business transactions, Coroners' courts were held in it and executors of wills paid out legacies. Sometimes a priest even held a small school for promising poor boys in the porch.

Sir James de Berners' widow, the Lady Anne, had the manor restored to her

The Medieval West Porch

in 1393, then in 1400 their young son, Sir Richard de Berners, came of age, and King Henry IV made a full grant of the manor to him. Lady Anne died three years later, and her son died six years after that. But, although he was only about 30 years old, he must have known he was dying, because he settled the manor on his wife, the Lady Phillipa and their only child, an infant called Margery, with four trustees to administer the estate, including William Weston of Albury and the Rector, John Denne.

There may have been tenants in the house at this time. After Sir Richard's death, Lady Phillipa married a second husband, Thomas Leukenore, but died soon afterwards. The young Margery was the sole heir and inherited the manor and its park, the free warren (hunting rights) and the advowson of the church. For convenience sake, she was made the child-bride of John Ferriby who held his first manor court in 1420 and sat in Parliament in 1425. They did not appear to have any children.

5

THE BOURCHIER FAMILY
1441-1536

In 1441 Margery's husband died. She was still quite young and later married Sir John Bourchier who was created the first Baron Berners shortly after the marriage. He was a great-grandson of Edward III and brother to the Archbishop of Canterbury, Cardinal Bourchier, who crowned Richard III in 1483. By this marriage, Margery had a son, Sir Humphrey Bourchier who grew up to marry Elizabeth Tilney. However, he was killed at the

Bourchier (Lord Berners)
1441-1536

battle of Barnet in 1471 during his father's lifetime. Altogether three members of the Bourchier family died at the Battle of Barnet. Beside this Sir Humphrey, there was another Humphrey Bourchier who was the first Lord Cromwell, and William, Viscount Bourchier. All were on Edward IV's victorious Yorkist side. Three years later Sir John Bourchier died and Margery in the following year. Their little grandson, another John Bourchier, was only eight years old when he inherited the manor. There did seem to be a preponderance of under age heirs to this manor. It must reflect the short lives most people had in the Middle Ages.

About the time of the death of the Bourchier's only son, Humphrey, at the battle of Barnet (1471), a chapel was built on the north side of the chancel. It may have been built especially as a chantry chapel for prayers to be said for his soul.

This chapel is joined on to the chancel by a wide archway which may have been created after the Reformation, and there is a south window with a flat-headed arch and three cinque foiled lights and a similar east window which is now hidden behind one of the memorials. There is a priest's doorway on the south wall which is also blocked. On the outside of this door can be seen the remains of a scratch dial on the right hand side. This has a hole in the middle for a metal gnomon and was a type of sun dial that told the priest when it was time for the services to begin.

There are still two wills surviving of this time. The first dated 1485 was of a parishioner called Humfrey Stynt (notice the fashion for being named after

25

those at the manor house!) He wished to be buried in St Mary's churchyard. He left four pence to the mother church of St Swithen at Winchester and 6s. 8d. for repairing the Holy Cross in St Mary's Church and the same amount for wax for candles in the chancel.

The other will was of a Sir Robert Rewmorgony who was a chaplain at Horsell and died in 1487 and wished to be buried in "the great chapel within the church of [West] Horsley". This suggests that he may have once been one of the rectors at St Mary's or perhaps a chantry chaplain. Although his name does not appear on the list of Rectors, there are believed to be several names missing during this period. This man only left two pence to the mother church of St Swithen, but the chief item in his will was his "long knife, the pommel with an eagle's claw gilt and also my hood of silk" which he left to an Edward Perpoynt.

Prosperity after Adversity

In the years following the Black Death (1349) West Horsley became a very prosperous village because it was involved with the wool trade. There is evidence that all the processes of cloth manufacturing were carried out here with the exception, perhaps, of dyeing. Although little was written down at this time, everything points to the fact that our village suffered badly during the Black Death. With so much land left untended afterwards, and so few peasants left to work the land, some of the better-off villagers, but mainly incomers, bought up the spare land and kept sheep on it. That was how the wool trade expanded in West Horsley and many other villages in Surrey. Several wool merchants and clothiers (cloth manufacturers) came to live here, which is the reason why we have so many large medieval houses still standing which were built at the end of the 14th century and beginning of the 15th century. Wix Farm, The Old Cottage (opposite West Horsley Motor Works), High Bank, Tunmore Farm, Sumners, and Lower Hammonds Farm are the main ones; when they were first built, they all belonged to wealthy people.

We have lost so many of the treasures out of our church that there is little to show where these wealthy people were buried, but it was probably under the floor in the nave. We know of two brasses that were stolen from the centre aisle and there may have been some others. Also the old floor has been taken up and relaid at least twice.

The 16th century was probably West Horsley's hey-day but in the 17th century with all the upheavals of the Civil War, came the rapid decline of the wool trade and West Horsley's part in it. Weavers were out of work and there was great poverty in country areas. This was the time when many of our old houses were first divided into two or more dwellings.

The Second Lord Berners 1474-1532

The orphaned John Bourchier, the second Lord Berners, inherited the manor in about 1474 when he was only eight years old, so it is probable that tenants were living in the manor house, and he may have been brought up at Court for he received a good education. He became both a distinguished soldier and a scholar and one of King Henry VIII's favourites. He was made Chancellor of the Exchequer for life and became renowned for his translation into English of Froissart's *Chronicles* which was published in 1526. (This was a 14th century work about the wars in which France, England and Spain had been engaged.)

This Lord Berners married Catherine Howard, a daughter of the Duke of Norfolk and they had two daughters, Margery and Joan. They lived mainly at Court and had an extravagant life-style, spending more than they could afford. King Henry granted Lord Berners several loans and gave him many manors, including those of Ockham, Effingham, Chipstead, Woldingham and others scattered around the Home Counties and Oxfordshire. But this was not enough to finance him. He mortgaged the "Manors of Westhorsselegh and Weke" (sic) and other manors in his possession. [Wix Farm was formerly a sub-manor of West Horsley, as was Lollesworth]. When he died in 1532 he was still heavily in debt to the king and, no doubt, many others.

Lord Berners' elder daughter having died young, his second daughter, Joan, was now his heiress. She had married Edmund Knyvett of Bukenham Castle in Norfolk, whose father had been Sergeant Porter to Henry VIII. Although Lord Berners stated in his will that three manors in Hertfordshire were to be given to the king after the death of his wife in settlement of a debt, Henry seized them without waiting for that lady's demise! She only managed to hold on to West Horsley which was still mortgaged and after her death, the king seized that, too!

6

THE COURTENAYS
1536-1539

King Henry then granted the manor of West Horsley to Henry Courtenay, Marquis of Exeter, together with Ockham and Effingham. This gentleman was a first cousin of Henry VIII, being the son of his aunt, Katherine Plantagenet. No further mention was ever made to the little manor of "Weke", so it must have been at this time that it became absorbed into West Horsley.

According to a book called *Henry VIII and his Court* by Neville Williams, King Henry visited his cousin soon after he moved into West Horsley House, as it was called then, and he gives the full menu for a dinner provided for the king and his entourage by the Marquis of Exeter. It is as follows:

"The first course consisted of salads of damsons, artichokes, cabbage lettuces, purslane and cucumbers, with which were served cold dishes of stewed sparrows, carp, capons in lemon, larded pheasants, duck, gulls, brews, forced rabbit, pasty of venison from fallow deer and pear pasty.

Henry Courtney
Marquis of Exeter
1536-1539

This was followed by a hot course of stork, gannet, heron, pullets, quail, partridge, fresh sturgeon, pasty of venison from red deer, chickens baked in caudle and fritters.

Once these dishes were removed, the third and last course was served, consisting of jelly, blancmange, apples with pistachios, pears with carraway, filberts, scraped cheese with sugar, clotted cream with sugar, quince pie, marchpane and rounded off with the customary wafers and hippocras, the cordial of spiced wine that was the Tudor equivalent of a glass of port."

According to the author, this was by no means a lavish repast compared with some of the banquets given at Whitehall for special embassies which led to the English acquiring a reputation for gluttony. Nevertheless, considering the size of the usual Royal entourage, the cost of the feast must have set the Marquis back a few pounds! And it doesn't say much for the King's loyalty to his cousin and childhood friend that five years later he should have him beheaded on flimsy evidence.

Nothing seems to have been done to the church during the time that the second Lord Berners held the manor. It is unlikely that he ever lived here and he was always in debt. Various dates have been suggested for the south aisle ranging from soon after the chapel was built to the early 16th century. Personally I think it must have been later than that, because, although the Marquis of Exeter definitely lived at West Horsley Place, he was here for such a short time that it is unlikely that he could have undertaken such a large task as building a new aisle onto the church. He was here during the time of the Dissolution of the Monasteries (1536) and the Reformation, when Chantry chapels became illegal and the worship of images and relics was forbidden, as was the sale of pardons. This could explain why the chapel had no dividing wall when the aisle was built and the chapel was opened out to be part of the aisle.

To form the aisle the south wall of the church was replaced with an arcade of four-centred arches on octagonal pillars, said to be rare in Surrey churches. These are similar to the arch between the chapel and the chancel. When the wall paintings were being investigated it was found that the south arcade had been decorated with post-Reformation black-letter texts within patterned borders. Possibly the north arcade was decorated in a similar fashion at the time.

There are three windows in the south aisle and in old prints of the church showing the south side, the third window can be seen to be of a much older date than the two square-headed Tudor windows. It is now no longer coeval with the date of the chapel (c.1470) but has been replaced since Cracklow made his drawing of the church in 1824. Both the original window and the one at the west end of the south aisle which are shown in this drawing, are older than the aisle itself. One could have been the west window of the chapel and the other could have come from the original south wall of the church. Mr Philip Mainwaring Johnston, an architect and antiquarian, puts the aisle at a later date than was previously thought, to the late 16th or even the first quarter of the 17th century. In which case the building of the south aisle must come into the Elizabethan period when either Lady Lincoln or Viscount Montague held the manor, but he was a Roman Catholic.

The Courtenays were only at West Horsley Place for about four or five years, so perhaps they did not have time to make any improvements to

Cracklow's drawing showing old window, second from the right

thechurch. However, their story is somewhat touching and worth recounting for it gives a good example of how delicately one had to tread at the Court of Henry VIII.

Henry Courtenay, Marquis of Exeter and Earl of Devonshire, was a first cousin of King Henry's and although he had served his cousin loyally as a prominent courtier and had assisted with the divorce of the first two Queens, he was a gentleman who enjoyed a merry life and was given to slight indiscretions which in the end were his undoing. Moreover, he mingled with "dangerous" company – that is to say, Roman Catholics – and soon found himself out of favour with the King's minister, Thomas Cromwell.

Exeter was "much given to singing merry songs in the Lady Marquis's garden at Horsley". These often took on treasonable overtones, being about the King's lady friends and certain delicate political matters. On one such occasion, Cromwell arrived unexpectedly on an uninvited visit and interrupted one of these songs in the garden at West Horsley Place. Exeter stopped singing and said with a touch of malice, though it was probably meant to be humorous, "Peace! Knaves rule about the king, I trust to give them a buffet one day."

Cromwell was not amused and ordered Exeter's immediate arrest. He managed to collect enough "evidence" to bring him to trial and condemn him to death together with two of his Catholic friends, on the pretext that they were plotting to overthrow the King and replace the Tudor line with the Yorkist line through Exeter himself, who was a direct descendant of Edward IV.

Knowing what a tightrope those at Court were walking may have been the reason why Exeter had settled the manors of West Horsley, Bishops Manor at East Horsley and two other manors in Ockham and Effingham, on his wife Gertrude a few years earlier. But little good that did, because Gertrude and their 12-year-old son, Edward, were also arrested and put in the Tower of London and all their estates were seized. After a brief trial, Exeter was beheaded on Tower Hill in December 1539 and was buried at St Mary's Essenden near Bedwell Park. The manor of West Horsley then reverted to Henry VIII and stayed in his possession until 1547, when he granted it to Sir Anthony Browne.

Gertrude Courtenay was a devout Catholic and was accused of holding traitorous correspondence with Cardinal Pole and other "dangerous" Catholics. She was confined to the Tower until the accession of the Catholic Queen Mary, who released her and made her a lady-in-waiting. The Queen also gave her an estate in Dorset to retire to. Lady Courtenay died in 1558 and was buried at Wimborne Minster.

The 12-year-old Edward was accused similarly with his parents, but the main reason for his imprisonment was probably because he was the last male descendant of the Plantagenet line, and was known as "the last sprig of the White Rose". When Mary came to the throne she also released young Edward, who would have been in his mid-twenties by this time, and restored the title of Earl of Devonshire to him. He was said to have good looks, charm and education, but lacked worldly experience and was rather a timid young man. Hardly surprising after having spent most of his life in prison!

There was a move afoot to marry Edward to Queen Mary who was 10 years his senior, but she was determined to marry her cousin, Philip of Spain. This was not popular with the people and there was a plot to depose the Catholic Mary and put 15-year-old Lady Jane Grey on the throne instead. She was the granddaughter of Henry VIII's younger sister, Mary Brandon. This plot failed and Lady Jane was executed.

Then another plot was hatched to marry Edward Courtenay to Princess Elizabeth, who was then aged about 20, and put them jointly on the throne. Fearing the executioner's block, Elizabeth kept a low profile at her house at Ashridge and Edward fled to Europe where he died of a fever in 1556. Thus ended the sad story of the Courtenays of West Horsley.

King Henry VIII 1539-1547

Henry VIII

We do not know if West Horsley House was occupied during the time that King Henry held the manor, but the house and garden must have been cared for, because two sets of accounts have come down to us relating to the upkeep of the garden during the last two quarters of 1546 and the first quarter of 1547 when it was the property of the Crown.

According to a bill from "John Gardyner, Keeper of the King's Garden at West Horsley", for the quarter ending Michaelmas, 1546, a total of £3 18s. 6d. was expended on garden upkeep. This included the wages for John Gardyner himself and for four labourers at 4d. per day, 3d. a day for weeders, 8d. paid to Richard Stynt for mowing the grass alleys and orchard and 10d. for two spades.

A further bill for the quarter ending with Christmas, gives the added expenditure, after the usual wages, for further wages for "picking and weeding out the knottes of the privy garden and of the mounte garden and out of the strawberry borders and roseers border".

Another bill of uncertain date stated that wages were paid for "setynge of knottes and Strawberry borders and for carrying of soil and earth to make the knottes in the mounte garden." We might wonder if this is the same knott garden that still exists today?

7

THE REFORMATION

Towards the latter part of the Middle Ages there was a great revival of learning which began in Italy in the 14th century and spread to the rest of Europe by the 16th century. It marked the end of the Middle Ages and the beginning of modern history. There was a rediscovery of classical literature and architecture, and more to the point, the invention of the printing press enabled people to read books for themselves which brought about a new freedom of thought, in contrast to the hitherto fixed teachings of the Church.

What is more, there was a new critical attitude towards religion, a general dissatisfaction with the Church of Rome, a common distaste of the worldliness and wealth of many of the clergy, and a desire to get back to the purity of teaching in the Bible. This in turn led to the emergence of several nonconformist movements.

Before we go on with our story about the patrons of St Mary's Church who lived at West Horsley Place, perhaps we should look at what happened in England after Henry VIII's split with the Church of Rome, and how the turbulent 16th and 17th centuries which followed, affected our church.

It is a well known fact that the main reason why Henry VIII broke away from the Roman Church in 1530 was because of his desire to divorce his queen, Katherine of Aragon. However, he was fairly conservative in the changes he made to religious services and the churches. The main difference was that the king was now head of the church instead of the Pope. In 1538 he made a rule that an English Bible must be placed in every church, and that people should learn the Lord's Prayer, the Ten Commandments and the Articles of Faith in English instead of Latin. However, on his death in 1547, more radical reformers, led by Archbishop Cranmer, introduced a stricter form of Protestantism into the English Church.

At the beginning of the 16th century St Mary's church was probably a typical medieval country church, with a huge Holy Rood (cross) hanging down from a massive beam (the two sawn-off ends can still be seen over the chancel arch). There would have been a wide gallery over the rood screen for the musicians, which was decorated with brightly painted effigies of the saints all picked out in gold; and over the gallery would be a picture of 'the Doom' or Last Judgement, which may have been on wood or painted directly onto the wall. And somewhere there would have been a niche or pedestal for a Madonna and Child.

All the other walls were painted with pictures illustrating Bible stories, as well as the huge St Christopher on the west wall, and there were also decorative masonry patterns with flowers and tendrils. The floor of the chancel would have been paved with decorative medieval tiles.

The statue of the Virgin Mary would have been one of the first things to go, together with the figure of Christ on the Holy Rood. This was to stop people worshipping them instead of God. The next step was to dismantle the huge rood screen and the gallery above with its effigies of saints. This may have been the time when the chancel arch was enlarged to its present size so that the congregation could see the priest in the chancel. Although it is of the Early English style, it has a much more sophisticated chamfer stop on the mouldings which dates it to at least the late 16th century. The present wooden screen and the screen into the chapel from the chancel were inserted at this time.

The wall paintings were limewashed over, which has helped to preserve them for us to see today, otherwise they would have completely faded by now. The more terrible iconoclasm did not occur until the reign of Charles I when the Puritans went round smashing up all the medieval stained glass. Luckily for us the two roundels, now over the altar, have survived, as has the figure of Sir James de Berners which is believed to be part of a much larger picture. Perhaps the other figures in the windows were saints which is why they were smashed.

There is no record of how many of our church's art treasures were lost at this time, but one thing we know for certain is that there was a medieval alabaster carved reredos or an altar front, dated about 1370, depicting the life of Christ, because a fragment of it was found beneath the floor when it was being renewed in 1810. This is now embedded in the chancel wall.

Also at this time, the church bells and church plate were taken by the Church Commissioners or were hidden by the churchwardens when news came of an imminent visit. In the 1930s when the tower of St Martin's, East Horsley was being renovated, some very old church silver was found behind some masonry in the wall.

Fragment of reredos

After the dissolution of the monasteries, some of the luckier inmates managed to become parish priests or tutors, but most received little or no compensation and were left to roam the country in abject poverty. Those who became parish priests had to obey the secular laws and become accustomed to altering their religion at the whim of the reigning monarch to whom they were now subject. In the smaller sphere of parish life, the squire also now became dominant over the parson, and any priest who would not bend to the changing tide of religious views lost his living.

In 1662 when the "Act of Uniformity" was passed, the clergy, who by this time were extremely nonconformist, were told to return to a new ritual in church services. Many refused and were ejected from their livings. Among these were John Platt of West Horsley and Sampson Carroll of East Horsley.

New laws also applied to the parishioners. During Elizabeth's reign there were two Acts of Uniformity which laid down that everyone must attend church services every Sunday, and if they refused to do so without a good excuse, they had to pay a fine of one shilling for each non-attendance. Many of the wealthier people just paid the fine, so it was later increased to £20 a month, an enormous sum in those days. Many of the nobility either went to prison or had their lands seized. Some even went abroad. Those who refused to attend, were those who still adhered to the Roman Catholic faith, and were called recusants. Several were reported by the churchwardens in East Horsley, but I am pleased to say that the churchwardens of West Horsley were less zealous in their duty, as only one was named, a certain Elizabeth Richbell who could not be fined because she had "departed this parish but whither we know not".

The chancel screen looking out into the nave. On the right are the Norman pillars of the north aisle. In the foreground can be seen the carved bench ends in the choir.

35

As chantry chapels were now illegal, the chapel on the south side of the chancel was stripped of everything that had been in it. Stone altars were ordered to be removed from the chancels of churches and replaced with wooden "Holy Tables" which were placed in the middle of the chancel away from the east wall.

During the brief reign of Queen Mary (1553-58) there was a return to ancient ritual and many of the images and relics which had been hidden reappeared in the churches. About a quarter of the clergy lost their livings because they would not return to Roman Catholicism but on the whole, the attempt at revival was a failure. So that when Elizabeth came to the throne in 1558, there was a smooth return to Protestant worship.

In 1570 the Pope excommunicated Queen Elizabeth for returning the country to Protestantism and sent Jesuit missionaries to try and re-convert the English people. Religious passions ran rife. By this time the common people with their hate of the Spanish, were staunchly Protestant and whenever a Jesuit was caught, he was hanged as a traitor. Catholic families hid priests in their houses in 'priest holes' which were constructed for the purpose. In West Horsley Place there is a little room which has a tiny window but appears to have no door. It is believed to be a priest hole, and as the family was Catholic it does seem highly likely to have been used for this purpose.

Newly appointed clergy were now strongly Protestant. Church services were reduced to two only – Morning Prayer and Evening Prayer. A reading desk was placed in the Nave facing the congregation from which the service was conducted by the priest, and the congregation in their turn made their own vocal contribution to the service.

There was a new Holy Communion service which took the place of Mass. In this the people went up to the Chancel and knelt around the Holy Table which was now draped in a cloth of some kind of rich material, often made out of the old vestments. On top of this was placed "a fair linen cloth". Participants took both bread and wine instead of only the bread as before.

Many of the parishes in England were held in plurality at this time and were usually looked after by a curate. In this parish, as the patrons of the church were Roman Catholic they could not present a Rector, and for a long time this was done by people whose connection with the village seems a bit obscure.

There was a general unstability regarding the appointment of priests, and the rules regarding their conduct lacked clarity. Some married during the young Edward VI's reign, but under Queen Mary this was not looked on with favour. However, in 1558 a ruling was made that priests could marry if the bride-to-be was first interviewed by the Bishop and two Justices of the Peace.

The exact dates are not known of the admission and departure of Thomas

Persons, Thomas Aspull and Robert Loughore, who were Rectors here between about 1477 and 1568. The last two named were probably non-resident, this is born out by the fact that wills at this time were witnessed by curates, instead of, as was customary, by the Parish Priest.

Robert Loughore was also Vicar of three parishes in Devon and was Archdeacon of Totnes (1562-1568), Chancellor of the Exeter Diocese, Official to the Archbishop of York and also M.P. for Pembroke. So it hardly seems possible that he had any time to visit his country parishes. One interesting fact we learn from the inventory of his goods after he died was that West Horsley parsonage was used as an inn for 'better class' travellers and the money went to poor relief.

Another interesting document in Guildford Muniment Room entitled "Complaints against a curate", dated 1576, gives us a picture of a very colourful character. His name was Martin Lory but the parishioners called him "Parson Newcut" because he was continually ordering new clothes in the latest style. He was a frequenter of houses of ill-repute in Guildford and had persuaded "Bicknell's wife of Merrow" to run away with him. He was a "very great swearer and a filthy talker." It was reported that he only came into the ministry for a change of position and intended to cast off the cloth when he had sold off two benefices he had acquired in the West Country. The report ended "... this behaviour is a discredit to his calling, sport to papists and a grief to honest men."

8

SIR ANTHONY BROWNE
AND THE MONTAGUES

After Henry Courteney was executed, West Horsley remained in the hands of the King for about nine years. Then he gave it to Sir Anthony Browne together with many other manors and vast tracts of land in Surrey which had once belonged to religious houses. Sir Anthony was a gentleman of the Privy Chamber, as had been Henry Courteney, and it says a lot for his diplomacy when we realize that he was one of the few survivors of the young contemporaries who had been appointed to the King's original Privy Council when he came to the throne, many of them having lost their heads.

King Henry must have felt that Sir Anthony was one of the few men whom he could trust, because he heaped many honours upon him. In 1539 he made him captain of the 'Gentlemen Pensioners'. This was a band of 50 young men of noble birth and good physique, well trained in the arts of war, who were to form an elite 'bodyguard'. Among them was Sir Nicholas Carew, a relation of Carew Raleigh, of whom we shall hear more later.

 In the same year, Sir Anthony was appointed Master of the Horse and King's Standard Bearer. He was a tutor to Princesses Mary and Elizabeth, and at the time that he came to West Horsley, he had been made guardian to the young Prince Edward and Princess Elizabeth. He must indeed have been a trusted and loyal servant.

Sir Anthony was married twice, his first wife, Alys

Sir Anthony Browne
1547-1552

Gage bearing him ten children before she died. Then as a widower, aged 60, he married a young girl of 15, the Lady Elizabeth FitzGerald.

Lady Elizabeth, the orphaned daughter of the 9th Earl of Kildare, was a second cousin to the Princesses Mary and Elizabeth and had been brought up with them as a companion, sharing their education.

When she was only 10 years old, Lady Elizabeth had been befriended by Henry Howard, Earl of Surrey who at the age of 26, as he was then, had already earned distinction as poet and soldier. He was captivated by the young girl's beauty and wrote his finest love lyrics to the "Fair Geraldine", as he called her. But to Surrey's disappointment, she was given in marriage to Sir Anthony.

Sir Edward & Lady Clinton
later Earl & Countess Lincoln
1552-1589

Lady Elizabeth was widowed when she was only 20, having had two children who both died in infancy. When she was 24 she became the third wife of Sir Edward Clinton, first Earl of Lincoln and by him had a large family. Edward Clinton's first wife, Bessie Blount, had been a cast-off mistress of Henry VIII's. She was the mother of the king's bastard son, Henry Fitzroy.

Edward Clinton died in 1585 and Lady Elizabeth lived out her widowhood at West Horsley House. During this time she kept up a correspondence with Sir William More of Loseley. In these letters she expressed her indignation at John Agmondesham of East Horsley attempting to enclose some of the common land in East Horsley to the detriment of the poor tenants; and in 1588, at the time of the Spanish Armada, she begged Sir William to come to her house to protect her in case the Spanish invaded.

Whilst Lady Elizabeth was lady of the manor, she obtained beech saplings from the Evelyn family at Wotton to plant out the beech avenue which led from the church and up the length of the Sheepleas to a house where the steward of the manor lived.

Lady Elizabeth died in 1589, six months after the defeat of the Armada, and West Horsley Manor passed to her stepson, a second Sir Anthony Browne, who had succeeded his father in 1548 and inherited the estates of Battle Abbey and Cowdray Park in Midhurst, Sussex. His first wife had died when giving birth to a son, but his second wife bore him seven children.

Although a staunch Roman Catholic, his loyalty to the Crown was above suspicion, and he enjoyed the confidence of both Edward VI and his sisters, Mary and Elizabeth. He had been M.P. for Guildford from 1542 to 1547, Petersfield in 1553 and for Surrey in 1554.

During the reign of the Catholic Mary Tudor, (1553-1558), Sir Anthony had honours heaped upon him. In 1554 on the occasion of Mary's marriage to Philip II of Spain, he was created the first Viscount Montague. (He chose that title because his grandmother, Lady Lucy, had been a daughter of John Neville, Marquis of Montacute, the spelling of which was a different version of the same name. He was also appointed Keeper of the Royal Parks.

On the accession of Elizabeth I, he lost his seat in the privy council because of his religious views. Nevertheless, he was employed two years later in 1561, on a special mission to the court of Spain, because the Queen held him in great esteem for his great prudence and wisdom. Then in 1587, because of his unshakable loyalty to the crown, and in spite of being a devout Roman

Catholic, he was one of the commissioners who sat at the trial of Mary, Queen of Scots.

Henley Park, near Guildford, was another of Viscount Montague's manors, where it is said, he frequently resided, and during those times it was notoriously the refuge of recusants (persons refusing to attend Church of England services) and suspected Jesuit priests. It is possible that the priest hole at West Horsley Place was constructed at this time.

Lord Montague, like his father before him, being a 'recusant', probably had to pay heavy fines for not attending church. Although, as he had so many houses, he would probably have managed to move about and dodge the churchwardens whose duty it was to name non-churchgoers. In spite of his religion, Queen Elizabeth was very fond of him and in 1592, when he was very ill and about to die, she came and visited him at West Horsley House. He was buried at Midhurst, which was where the principal family seat, Cowdray Place, was situated.

After the death of the first Lord Montague in 1592, the estate was inherited by his son Anthony Maria Browne, 2nd Viscount Montague of Cowdray. As a Member of Parliament, he was committed in November 1605 on charge of complicity in the aims of the gunpowder plot to blow up the Houses of Parliament, the only evidence being that he was absent on that fateful day. He was apparently guilty of nothing worse than being a known Roman Catholic. Nevertheless, he was imprisoned in the Tower of London until the following August. Unable to find him guilty, the court fined him £200 and allowed him to go free. Later in 1611 he was pardoned of all fines for recusancy on paying a lump sum of £6,000. He died in 1629 at Horsley House, and was succeeded by his son Francis, the 3rd Viscount Montague, aged 19.

The young Viscount was soon in debt and had to mortgage the estate to John Evelyn of Wotton and others. But his troubles did not stop there. Being both a Roman Catholic and a Royalist, his estates were continually plundered and finally sequestrated by the Parliamentarians at the beginning of the Civil War in 1642. West Horsley House was then bought by the brother-in-law of Sir Walter Raleigh, Sir Nicholas Throckmorton, who was the nephew and heir

Sir Nicholas Throckmorton
1642–1643

to Sir Francis Carew of Beddington, and took his uncle's surname and coat of arms when he died in 1607. Sir Nicholas died in 1643 and left West Horsley Manor to his sister's son, Carew Raleigh who had been born in the Tower of London when his father, Sir Walter Raleigh was imprisoned there. After Sir Walter was executed the family had their remaining estates confiscated, so Carew Raleigh brought his mother and wife and children to live at West Horsley House.

40

9

THE SEVENTEENTH CENTURY

Sir Walter Raleigh (1552-1618)

Although Sir Walter Raleigh never lived in West Horsley, his head was brought here after his execution by his wife, and remains under the floor of the side chapel in St Mary's Church. It seems worthwhile pausing at this point in our narrative to give a short account of the life of this great and versatile man.

Sir Walter Raleigh was born in Devon but little is known of his formative years until he went to France in 1569 with a cousin to join a band of gentleman volunteers to fight on the Protestant side in the Wars of Religion.

In 1572 he went up to Oriel College, Oxford, but did not stay to take his degree. Three years later he enrolled at the Middle Temple in the Inns of Court. But again he did not stay the course, for in 1778 he joined his half-brother, Sir Humphrey Gilbert, in a scheme to explore and colonise the coast of North America. Later that same year, Gilbert led a piratical expedition against the Spaniards and Raleigh accompanied him as captain of a ship called the 'Falcon'.

Back in England in 1580, Raleigh became a hanger-on at court and attached himself to the Earl of Leicester, while he waited for a new mission. In that year, he was twice arrested for fighting duels and was soon sent off to fight more usefully in Europe and Ireland.

In 1581 he was sent home with despatches to the Queen, and she is said to have been attracted by his reckless courage, his excellent manners and his sumptuous clothes. He is said to have been a tall handsome man with dark curly hair and piercing blue eyes. The story that has come down to us about Raleigh spreading his new cloak over a muddy place so the Queen would not soil her shoes is believed to be true, and she is said to have rewarded him with several new cloaks. The deed must have drawn the Queen's attention to him for he quickly joined the innermost circle of courtiers and soon became one of her favourites. Moreover, Raleigh was a natural poet and flattered the Queen with several poems he wrote to her.

The Queen granted him several administrative appointments and also Sherborne Castle in Dorset. He became one of the richest men in England, but soon began spending his wealth in the Queen's service, mounting several expeditions of exploration. After Sir Humphrey Gilbert was lost at sea in 1583, Raleigh took over his leading role in the attempt to found an English colony in America. The result was 'Virginia', which he named after the 'Virgin Queen'. As a reward she bestowed a knighthood upon him. Exploration continued as his chief occupation for many years, and the discovery of the potato and tobacco have been attributed to him.

After 1587, Raleigh's place as favourite at Court was being usurped by the Earl of Essex, and in about 1591 he enraged the Queen when she discovered that he had secretly married one of her ladies-in-waiting, Bess Throckmorton. Raleigh had already set out on yet another expedition when the Queen heard about it and she sent a fast ship to reach him off the coast of Spain with orders for him to return at once. Both Raleigh and his now pregnant wife, were put in the Tower of London in separate custody, and, too late, Raleigh affected extravagant grief and self-abasement, all to no avail. The Queen was unmoved. After nearly a year the couple were released from the Tower, where their first born son had died.

Now being excluded from Court, they retired to Sherborne, where Raleigh began to renovate the old castle. But soon he changed his mind and had a new house built nearby. Here their second son was born in 1594 and was named Walter after his father. However, domestic life did not suit Raleigh's restless spirit and he began planning a new expedition to discover the fabled land called El Dorado in South America, which he hoped would restore him to the Queen's favour. On his return he brought back news of the Indian's hostility towards the Spanish and hoped the Queen would mount an expedition with him in command to seize the territory from the Spanish. Instead, she put him in charge of a squadron to intercept Spanish treasure ships off the Azores.

Queen Elizabeth died in 1603 and James I arrived in England to become king. Raleigh was soon accused of treason with other conspirators of trying to dethrone the new king, and making Lady Arabella Stuart Queen in his place. She was the great-granddaughter of Margaret Tudor, a sister of Henry VIII's, also a cousin of James I's. The case against Raleigh was unproven, so he was spared the block   but remained in the Tower of London for 12 years. This time however, he was allowed several comforts. He had the use of the Bloody

Tower and the adjoining garden, he was allowed servants, a physician and a clergyman, and his wife was allowed to stay with him and come and go as she pleased. In 1605 another son was born to them in the Tower. He was baptised Carew after his godfather, Richard Carew.

Raleigh spent his time growing herbs which he distilled into medical cordials and he embarked on his 'History of the World'. In the meantime, Sherbourne Castle, which he hoped to secure for his elder son, Walter, was confiscated. In his desperation to get out of prison, Raleigh made wild promises to the king that he could secure gold mines in South America for him. So, on this condition the king released him.

To finance this new venture Raleigh sold his last possession, a manor in Mitcham which was his wife's dowry, and with his son Walter beside him he set off for the Orinoco River. But the expedition was a failure, they ran into a Spanish settlement and a battle ensued during which his son was wounded and died soon after. They lost their way to the mines, as they had no maps and certain landmarks had disappeared, and so had to abandon the quest.

Raleigh returned to England and was immediately arrested and sentenced to death for fighting the Spanish, in order to further King James' policy of friendship towards the Spanish. He was imprisoned in the gatehouse of the Old Palace at Westminster and sentenced to be executed in the Old Palace yard. Raleigh's last visitor was his wife and she told him she had received permission to bury his body at the nearby church of St Margaret's, whereupon he joked that she now had control over his body as she never had during his life.

On the morning of the execution in October 1618, Raleigh donned his finest clothes, refused a blindfold and gave a long speech. It took two blows to sever his head. Normally a traitor's head was placed on a spike on London Bridge, but for some reason, perhaps because Sir Walter was a popular hero of the people, his head was put in a red leather bag, bundled up in his cloak and secretly given to Lady Raleigh as she drove away in her carriage. She had it embalmed and kept it beside her until her death, 29 years later. It then passed into the keeping of her son Carew.

Lady Raleigh begged that she might keep her husband's library, globes, scientific instruments and manuscripts which had never been printed. But the King's Commissioners pounced on everything indiscriminately, with the excuse that they would be of "small use to Sir Walter's wife". They themselves made no use of them and very soon all his unprinted writings were lost. The Commissioners also seized Sir Walter's last ship, the 'Destiny' with everything in it. They only paid back to Lady Raleigh the sum of money she had put into it from the sale of her own estate.

Lady Raleigh and her young son Carew, then aged about 13, were saved from penury by her husband's friends and relatives. They saw that the boy was well educated and then introduced him to Court.

When Carew Raleigh came to West Horsley Place with his family, he brought his mother here to live with them. After her death the story passed down the centuries by old retainers at "The Place", was, that Sir Walter's head was kept in a cupboard in the hall.

Carew Raleigh (1605-1665)

Carew Raleigh, the youngest and only surviving child of Sir Walter Raleigh, was educated at Wadham College, Oxford. He was later introduced to Court by a kinsman, the Earl of Pembroke, but King James I (who was responsible for the execution of his father) took an instant dislike to him, saying he was "like his father's ghost". Carew sensed a hint of danger and immediately left the country to embark on foreign travel.

Carew Raleigh
1643 -1665

King Charles I was kinder to him and in 1623, restored some of his family inheritance on condition that he resigned all claim to Sherbourne Castle and its estate which King James I had given to Sir John Digby. Also about this time, he married Lady Philippa Weston, who was the rich young widow of Sir Anthony Ashley. These two facts must have enabled him to buy Bishop's Manor in East Horsley in 1629, from the Earl of Southampton.

Carew had made a name for himself at Court by performing in Ben Johnson's masque, 'Love's Triumphs' and in 1635 he was appointed a Gentleman of the Privy Chamber. But four years later, he blotted his copybook by drawing his sword on a fellow courtier, which resulted in suspension from duties and a week in the Fleet prison. It would seem that he had inherited his father's quick temper as well as his looks.

West Horsley House and its estate had been bought by Carew Raleigh's uncle, Sir Nicholas Carew (formerly Throckmorton) in about 1642 or 1643 from the impoverished Catholic 3rd Viscount Montague, whose fortunes fell victim to the Civil War. However, he was not to enjoy the property himself, for he died shortly afterwards and left it to his nephew.

There is nothing to suggest that the Raleighs actually lived in Bishop's Manor, which was theirs for about 15 years. They may well have stayed there from time to time when they were not at Court, but they certainly made a home for themselves at West Horsley House, and lived there throughout the Civil War. It was their main residence for about 21 years, and a few years after inheriting it, they sold Bishop's Manor to Sir Henry Hildeyard.

Some sources say that it may have been the 3rd Viscount Montague who was responsible for at least some of the rebuilding work at West Horsley House, on the evidence that he had secured a mortgage from the diarist, Mr John Evelyn of Wotton, but that may have been because he was heavily in debt. It seems more logical to suppose that Carew Raleigh, having recently come

44

into money, would be the more likely candidate for the restyling and partial rebuilding of the house, including the erection of the Jacobean staircase between the Great Hall and the west wing. There is a sentence in the Nicholas papers which states that Carew Raleigh spent £2,000 on improvements to the house! A vast sum of money when you consider that he sold the house and the whole estate, including the sub manors of Wix and Lollesworth for a mere £9,750.

West Horsley House was (and most of it still is) a timber-framed medieval house, which is what Bishop's Manor had been, but on a smaller scale. The previous owners of Bishop's Manor, the Cornwallises, had faced the house with brick and built two new wings in order to give it the appearance of a new Elizabethan house. This may have inspired Carew to give the same treatment to West Horsley House. One theory is that it had originally been a medieval courtyard house with the buildings arranged around a square, with at least two gateways leading into it. This is borne out by two field names; the one to the east was called Brewhouse Close and the one in front was called Court-house Gate. Many medieval manor houses were built around a courtyard with two or more entrances into it. Apart from the private apartments, and guest suites, a courthouse would have been incorporated into the buildings where the manorial courts would have been held, as well as the usual domestic offices, such as brew house, kitchens, bakehouse, and laundry.

Raleigh must have pulled down all the old service buildings, faced the front with brick and added on the "new" kitchen wing to the other side of the great hall to give it a balanced and more classic appearance. The advantage of West Horsley Manor over Bishop's Manor was that, apart from the house being larger, the park around it and also the estate were also very much larger, and it seems clear that Carew was hoping to make it his main family seat as King Charles I had also refused to give him back the former family home, Sherbourne Castle.

West Horsley Place after Carew Raleigh had partially rebuilt it and restyled it giving the whole house a new front. The remaining medieval wing is on the left.

Raleigh could have been responsible for the present layout of the gardens, but the building of the famous serpentine wall, sometimes called a 'crinkle-crankle', which is a rare feature in this part of England, may have been carried out by the next owner.

The Raleigh family lived here between 1643 and 1664, during the years of the Civil War and the Commonwealth, and during this period Carew became a Member of Parliament; between 1648 and 1653 he represented Haslemere and from 1658 to 1659 he represented Guildford. In 1650 he spent a few days in the Tower of London, the place of his birth, after another display of hot temper.

Several of the Raleighs' children were born while they lived at West Horsley and on 10th August 1658, John Evelyn records in his diary "I dined at Mr Carew Raleigh's at Horsley, son of the famous Sir Walter".

At the Restoration of the Monarchy in 1660, Carew was offered a knighthood by King Charles II, but embittered because he also refused to return Sherbourne Castle to him, he declined the honour in favour of his eldest son, Walter.

Shortly after this in the same year, tragedy struck the family in the shape of an epidemic. The two elder boys, Walter and Carew died and also a four-month-old daughter called Henereta (sic). There is no record of what the epidemic was – smallpox, typhus and plague were rife at the time, but it is unlikely to have been plague, because they were buried in the side chapel of St Mary's Church, which had formerly been a chantry chapel. This would not have been allowed had it been the plague.

It may have been at this time, in 1660, that Sir Walter Raleigh's head was retrieved from its cupboard and interred under the floor of the side chapel of the church with the bodies of his children.

The Raleighs now had only two children left, a young daughter and a small son called Philip, and the blow seemed to have taken the heart out of them. In 1664 they sold the estate to Sir Edward Nicholas and went to live in their London house in St Martin's Lane.

Three years later, Carew died a mysterious death and mystery surrounds the exact place of his burial. Initially he was buried in St Margaret's, Westminster where the register records that he had been "kild", which suggests either that he was murdered or perhaps was killed in a duel fought after another loss of temper. However, rumour had it that thirteen years later, in 1680, his body was removed and re-buried in the family grave at St Mary's Church, but there is no reference to this in the Parish Records.

As to St Mary's Church itself, little structural change seems to have been made to it in this century, except that a new porch was built on the north side of the church, which may have been to replace a medieval one similar to the west porch.

The original church bells could have been taken away at the time of the

Reformation, because all three of the present bells were placed in the tower in the 17th century and may have been donated by church patrons. They were made by a family of bell-founders at Weybridge and are dated 1621, 1645 and 1687.

The oldest tomb in the churchyard is a table tomb dated 1699. It stands in the north-west corner of the church. The inscription is now illegible but was recorded in the last century as being the tomb of Damaris Luffe, wife of Richard Luffe, yeoman, who lived at Highbank on Butler's Hill. It is possible that this man's family had made their wealth from wool. Table tombs are said to have been used to dispense bread and beer to the poor of the parish. Until that time, only the wealthy were buried in coffins, everyone else being laid in the ground in only a shroud, and graves in the churchyard had not been marked with anything more lasting than wood, but it was at this time that 'barrel graves' were coming in for the wealthier parishioners and several to the east and south-east of the chancel date from this time. These graves were brick-lined and had a barrelled roof made of brick, plus a headstone and footstone.

*An old drawing of the church, dated 1809, showing
the old north aisle and the Jacobean porch*

47

These are the only drawings known to exist of the Old Rectory before it was altered in 1819. Below is the front or south side and above is the back or north side which faces onto the farmyard.

John Platt, Minister of this Parish 1647-1662

Before leaving the period when the Raleighs were at West Horsley Place, it seems worth writing about another notable clergyman – John Platt, who was here between 1647 and 1662. It was during the latter part of the Civil War, the execution of Charles I, Oliver Cromwell's Protectorate, the Commonwealth and finally the Restoration of the Monarchy. They were momentous times in the history of England.

John Platt was **not** presented to the living by the patron, Carew Raleigh. He was an extreme non-conformist, preferring to be styled "Minister". It is said that he was appointed against the parishioners' wishes and he sounds like a hard man.

Little is known of him until he married Margaret Gavell, widow of Vincent Gavell, lord of the Manor of Cobham, whose seat was at Cobham Court. Margaret's son was a small child at the time, and John Platt assumed the duties of lord of the manor until the boy came of age. They leased Cobham Court to a tenant and came to live at the Parsonage House, as it was called then, in West Horsley which is now the present house called the Old Rectory. At that time, the house was timber framed and probably dated from the late 14th century like the tithe barn behind it, but the wing at the back dates from the mid-seventeenth century and most likely was built at the time the Platts were here.

While they were in this parish, John Platt's wife, Margaret, bore him five children: Elizabeth (1647), John (1649), Mary (1651), Humphrye (1653) and Sarah (1655). Also while they were here, he sold the malthouse on 'Burtley Hill' (Butlers Hill), but it is not clear if this was his own property or if it belonged to the church, which still owned the Red Lion Inn next door to St Mary's.

The church registers were not well kept during John Platt's ministry, with only a few entries made, and those usually of notable people. In one year, for instance, in the baptisms only one entry was made – that of his daughter Elizabeth. Whether this was because all the able-bodied men had been pressed into the militia the previous year and no babies were born, or whether there was no one left to carry out church duties who could write, is not known. But one would assume it was the duty of the Minister to see the registers were kept up-to-date. Perhaps he was too busy with his other duties as lord of the Manor of Cobham. One significant entry which is missing is the death of Sir Walter Raleigh's widow in 1647, but perhaps she was buried elsewhere.

During the Civil War and immediately after it, there was a great deal of poverty and a movement called "the Diggers" or "The True Levellers" was formed by the landless poor who took over parts of commons or waste ground and ploughed them up to grow crops to support themselves and their families. They were inspired by the writings of a man called Gerrard Winstanley who was a Quaker and lived in Cobham. I often wonder if we had "Levellers" in West Horsley, because on the Downs near the Upper Common there was a

Illustration from 'The True Levellers Standard'. Printed in 1649

field called "Lowlers Ride" – "ride" meaning "ridden of trees", and "Lowler" could be how the word leveller has come down to us in the vernacular.

In his capacity as lord of the manor of Cobham, John Platt was instrumental in finally wrecking the "Digger" movement at Cobham and destroying their crops and the huts they had built, so that they were left without shelter and without any food. Moreover he turned the people of Cobham against them, saying the Diggers would take away their common land from them, so they would have nowhere to graze their animals. This meant the shop-keepers would not sell them any food and they were hounded out of the village. It probably sounds strange to us today that a non-conformist minister should be against the poor trying to fend for themselves, but it seems that he was a landowner first and a minister of the church second!

In 1661 John Platt was a juryman and one of the "Triers of Clergy" for Surrey. In the following year the new king Charles II, passed an "Act of Uniformity" which stated that all clergy were required to accept the new book of Common Prayer and return to the ritual of church services. Many refused, and among them were John Platt and Samson Carroll of East Horsley and both were ejected from their livings.

Samson Carroll retired to a house (now rebuilt) which stood next to "The Old Cottage" opposite Sheppard's Garage. It was owned by the church and was a house where curates sometimes lived. It was about this time that Platt's stepson, Robert Gavell, came of age and inherited the manor of Cobham, so when the Platts left Horsley they bought the Manor of Westbrook in Godalming to retire to.

10

THE NICHOLAS FAMILY
1665-1749

Sir Edward Nicholas 1665-1667

Sir Edward Nicholas, who had bought the West Horsley estate from Carew Raleigh, had been Secretary to the Duke of Buckingham until 1628 and then became First Secretary to Charles I. He was knighted in 1641, and after the king was executed in 1649, he went into exile with the future King Charles II. After the Restoration of the Monarchy, he resumed the post of First Secretary until ill-health and advancing years forced him to retire in 1665 to the house he had bought in Horsley.

Nidjolas Family
1665-1749

The king offered Sir Edward a peerage, but he refused it, and it is reputed that the king visited him here at Horsley shortly before he died in 1667. His widow,Dame Jane (née Jay), lived on for another 19 years. They had four sons and four daughters. John Evelyn the diarist who was a friend of the family, wrote in his diary on 16th September 1665, the year of the Great Plague, … [I went] "to visite old Secretary Nicholas, being now at his new purchase of West Horsley, once mortgag'd to me by Lord Visct. Montagu: a pretty drie seate on the Downe."

Sir John Nicholas 1667-1704

Sir Edward Nicholas was succeeded by his eldest son John, who had also attended Charles II in exile. He was made Knight of the Bath and appointed Clerk of the Council, an office which he retained until the days of Queen Anne. He died in 1704.

Sir John was a careful, precise man and carried his clerkly habits into his private life, jotting down expenses, rents and memoranda into many small books. One entry was about the great storm of November 26, 1703 and the death of his wife, the Lady Penelope Compton, daughter of the Earl of Northampton: "This night was the dreadful storm and tempest wherin my

51

deare wife was killed in our bed by the fall of the chimney, and I was wonderfully preserved by God's Providence." Sir John died a year later.

When a grave was being dug for Lady Penelope in the chapel at St Mary's church, their son William was supervising operations when Sir Walter Raleigh's skull was uncovered. It lay beside the grave of the young Carew Raleigh in a small hole in the chalky floor not large enough to contain a body. This is the last time it was seen.

Sir John and Lady Penelope Nicholas had three sons, Edward, John and William and a daughter called Penelope. The eldest son, Edward, was Treasurer to Queen Mary, Joint-Regent with William III, and much of his correspondence with her is now in the British Museum. When his father died he inherited the manor, but he and his wife, Rachel, had no children. So when he died at Bath in 1726, whilst 'taking the waters', his brother John inherited the estate.

William Nicholas 1742-1749

John Nicholas had married his cousin Bridget and had three daughters but no sons by the marriage, so when he died the estate passed to the youngest brother, William, who died unmarried in 1749 at the ripe age of 81. William, like the rest of the family, was well educated and had a wide range of interests including art, mathematics, astronomy, history and horticulture among many other subjects, and he left many papers and notes on his researches and discoveries.

The Nicholas family of West Horsley will be remembered by the collection of letters, diaries and other manuscripts which together form the "Nicholas Papers". These came into the possession of the Evelyn family at Wotton after the death of William and eventually were passed to the British Museum, but many of the original papers are lost and only transcripts remain.

The Nicholas family also made changes to West Horsley Place: the stable block was built in 1669 and many of the rooms were decorated in the Georgian style. They also erected the beautiful wrought-iron gates and probably the famous serpentine wall in the kitchen garden, known as the "crinkle-crankle" wall, which was used for sheltering tender fruit trees, such as peaches and nectarines.

In October 1743, Sir John Evelyn, the son of the diarist, wrote a letter from Edinburgh addressed to "William Nicholas, Esqre, at West Horsley near Ripley in Surrey". In it he commented on the fine weather in Scotland and, referring to a letter he had had recently from Mr Nicholas, he wrote "that the fruit at Horsley should be so good this year is no wonder to us." This letter is doubly interesting because, apart from suggesting the serpentine wall was already in use, it tells us that a posting inn at Ripley, which was The Talbot, was the place from where mail had to be collected for West Horsley in the days before the penny post was introduced.

Other letters and papers belonging to William Nicholas were on such diverse and widely differing subjects as a "Computation of the Cistern in the Pump House at The Place", the "Planting of Fruit Trees against Walls", the "Sale of Timber", the "Manner in which Wheat Grows", the "Velocity of Sound", "the Circumference of the Earth" and the most telling of all – "the Happiness of the Unmarried" to name but a few! Even though he managed to remain "happily" unmarried until his death, William had an illegitimate daughter called Anne Copperthwaite whom he provided for by making her his heiress. She later married Sir Henry Weston of Ockham, but more of that later.

The Nicholas Chapel

The chapel to the south of the chancel in St Mary's Church which had once been a chantry chapel and in which the Raleigh children were buried, now became the Nicholas family pew and no doubt contained comfortable seats and footstools and was curtained off from the rest of the congregation. The floor was laid with black and white marble tiles and a fretted pine screen was added between it and the south aisle.

Detail from tracery of screen

The chapel became known as "The Nicholas Chapel" because the family memorials were placed around the walls and members of the family were buried beneath the floor. There is no crypt, just solid chalk in which the graves were dug. It is not known if there were any memorials in the chapel before this time, either to the Raleighs or any of the previous owners of West Horsley Place, for if there were, they are lost to us now.

Sir John and Lady Penelope Nicholas and their son Edward were buried under the floor of the chapel. Their son John and his wife Bridget were buried outside the chapel wall in a large white marble table tomb surrounded by railings, and the youngest son, William was buried in a low table tomb close by his brother's.

In 1678, in order to try and revive the declining wool trade, an Act of Parliament had been passed making it a law that all deceased persons must be buried in wool only. This law was enforced for 136 years and an affidavit stating the person had been buried in wool had to be produced for each burial, otherwise there was a penalty of £5 to be paid. The wealthy regarded this as a tax on funerals and preferred to pay up rather than conform. Most of the

Nicholas family were buried in either linen or velvet-lined coffins, so they had to pay this fine.

The Manor

The Nicholas family's habit of being meticulous in their accounts and writing of memoranda reflects also in the Manorial Court records and Church accounts. From these we learn many interesting little anecdotes to do with the day-to-day running of the estate.

One such interesting item was that, differing from many other manors, there had been an age-old custom in West Horsley for tenants to have the right to dig sand and cut timber on their holdings and to cut bushes and beat down acorns on the waste land. The steward to the manor, William Dawson, however, was ignorant of this custom and after several attempts to fine tenants for doing these things, wrote a letter in 1709 to his employer confessing his inability to settle these matters and asking for direction as to how he should proceed, because the issue came up regularly at every sitting of the Court Barron. Unfortunately, there is no record of the reply he received, but two years later a jury at the Court Barron fixed penalties for "any who beat oaks for acorns", so perhaps some of the customs were dis-

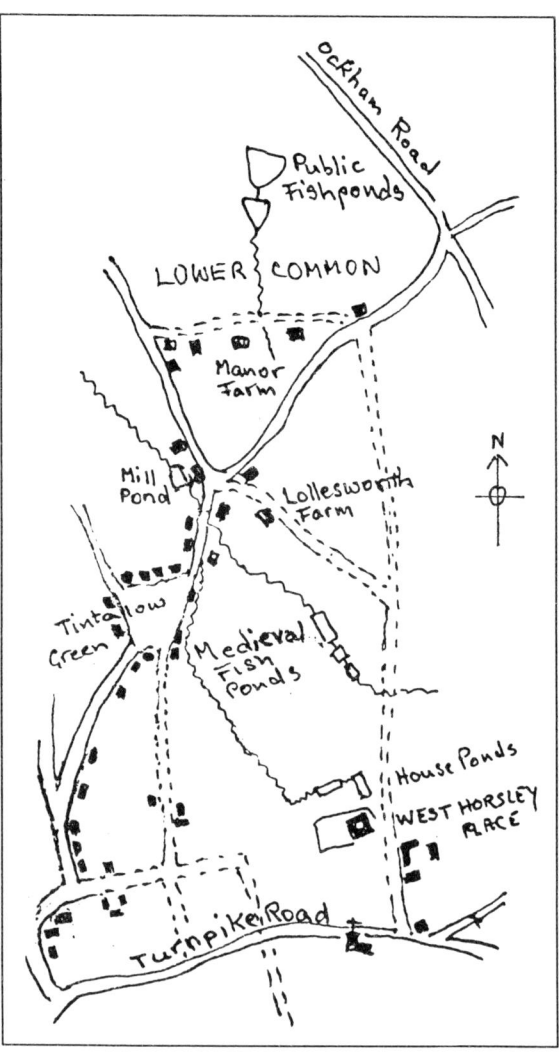

allowed.

There are numerous bills for work carried out on the manor, incorporating some imaginative and amusing spelling, and they give us a good insight into contemporary wages and cost of materials. We also find out that the "heriot" system was still in use, whereby on the death of a tenant, his best beast had to be given to the Lord of the Manor and the second best beast had to be given to the Church. This was a form of death duty, but after the Reformation the Church's claim gradually petered out.

We also learn that a brickyard existed at Ockham because a brickmaker called Nicholas Yearly of Ockham, bought a considerable number of beech trees at different times from Henley Copse, Hookwood and Henley Shrubb, all in West Horsley. These would have been used to fire the furnaces in the brick kilns.

One interesting memorandum written in 1718 by Mr Edward Nicholas says: "I tooke out of ye Lower Parke pond 62 carps and 150 perch which I put into ye upper pond in ye Comon. I alsoe put in 23 carps from ye square pond and ten perch. I put alsoe into ye square pond 3 carps, some tench and a bushell of perch."

This tells us that the medieval fish ponds behind West Horsley Place were still in use at the beginning of the eighteenth century and that fish was still being transported to the ponds on the Lower Common from where they were sold to the public. Only one pond on the former common is still in existence; it is incorporated into the camp site off Ockham Road North. There were actually three medieval ponds behind West Horsley Place, one oblong and two square – perhaps in Mr Nicholas' day one was already disused. They are now dry and overgrown with trees but their outline can be seen clearly.

The Church and Clergy

During most of the 18th century there was a spiritual deadness in the Church. Morality rather than doctrine was preached and an indifference was shown to church buildings and their contents. Holy Communion was usually only celebrated once a quarter and the number of communicants was extremely low. Church chancels were only used for these quarterly services and so fell into disrepair and often became a depository for lumber. A Bishop's Visitation report in 1711, tells us that St Mary's was one of these neglected churches.

The clergymen of the period were usually better educated than in previous centuries and were often the younger sons of squires and minor gentry and were given a benefice, or even multiple benefices, in order to provide them with a living. In 1718 the valuation of the West Horsley benefice was £200 a year. Little is known about most of the actual incumbents of this parish during this period, but one was Nathaniel Gower who was also the Vicar of Battersea. He was seldom at either of these two parishes, it is not even known what the names of his curates were. He was presented to the parish in 1711 by his friend Edward Nicholas and died at Bath in 1727 where he resided on account of his health. It seems that Edward Nicholas also went to Bath at fairly frequent intervals, and he died there, too.

We know a little more about Adam Langley M.A. who was the next incumbent at St Mary's. He was married in this parish and six of his children were baptised here so he must have resided here for much of the time, in spite of also being rector of St Matthew's, Friday Street in London. Of one of his curates, Henry Venn, we know even more, because he was the subject of a biography.

Henry Venn came of a long line of clergymen and won a scholarship to Jesus College, Cambridge. After his ordination he began his church career at the age of 26 years as Adam Langley's curate. His duties were to serve St Matthew's church in London during part of the summer and to reside for the remaining year in West Horsley. It is said that Henry Venn was very fond of cricket while at Cambridge, but after he was ordained he never played again.

While he was in West Horsley, he apparently instructed many of the poor on weekdays at his own home. His family prayers were attended by 30 or 40 poor neighbours and the number of communicants at the church increased from 12 to 60. He spent much of his time in reading, in meditation, in prayer, and in seeking after perfection. It is not surprising in view of the state of the church at the time that neighbouring clergy regarded him as an enthusiastic crank, more suited to the Methodist Chapel than the Church of England. He was at West Horsley for only four years from 1750 to 1754, but he must have made quite an impression on the poor of the parish, for at that time the clergy were regarded as being on a par with "the gentry" – to be looked up to but not to be spoken to without just cause!

Henry Venn then moved on to become curate of Clapham and eventually Vicar of Huddersfield. He became one of the great evangelising Christians and made an impression on people wherever he went.

11

THE WESTON FAMILY
1749-1921

The Weston family originated in Ashurst and Ifield in Sussex before coming to Albury in Surrey. But by the 15th century they no longer owned these estates but instead held estates in West Clandon, Send and Horsham, together with some land in Ockham which they had acquired through marriage. Several generations later, a Henry Weston who had descended from the original Ashurst family, bought the manor of Ockham from Richard Weston of Sutton Place, who was not a relation, his family having come from Lincolnshire.

Weston Family
1749-1921

This Henry Weston died in 1615 and the estate passed first to his brother, then his nephew, Sir Henry Weston, then to his great-nephew, Richard Weston, both of whom served as High Sheriff for Surrey and Sussex. Richard Weston also acted as Receiver General for the county which resulted in him being imprisoned for debts to the Crown. In 1710, when his son Henry came of age, the two of them set about selling the Ockham estate in order to pay off the debts, and when this was accomplished their former wealth was greatly diminished.

In spite of this unfortunate state of affairs, Henry must have been well liked among the local gentry, because two of them left Henry handsome legacies in the form of property at Chertsey: Sir William Perkins of Chertsey appointed him as his executor and residuary legatee, and another neighbour, Captain Matthew Perkins, also left him property. Then when he was in his late sixties, Henry Weston married the illegitimate daughter of William Nicholas, Anne Copperthwaite, and became the heir to the West Horsley estate.

William Nicholas did not die until 1749, and when Henry Weston inherited West Horsley, he was nearly seventy. His wife had died earlier in the same year when she gave birth to their second child, a son who was christened Henry Perkins. They already had a daughter born in 1747 and the couple must have been living at West Horsley Place when William Nicholas was still alive, because when Anne died she was buried at St Mary's and a note in the Burial

Register said she was buried in linen and "£5 was paid into Mr William Nicholas' hands for ye use of ye poor of this Parish."

Henry Weston drew up plans to completely rebuild West Horsley Place in the classic manner that was fashionable at the time. But when he showed the plans to the Duke of Marlborough, that gentleman asked him "Pray, Mr Weston, how old are you?" Henry took the hint and contented himself with alterations to the interior only.

The young Henry Perkins Weston was only 10 years old when his father died in 1759, and two guardians were appointed to look after him and administer the estate. One of these was his cousin, John Fullerton, whom his father had instituted as Rector of St Mary's in the previous year. But the young Henry turned out to be somewhat of a gambler and lost much of the family property. He chose to live in Lausanne, Switzerland for most of the time on the Rovereux estate which he had acquired through marrying a Swiss heiress, Marianne Bergier de Rovereux. Their wedding took place in St Mary's church, West Horsley, in 1770.

Henry Perkins and Marianne had five children: Henry Benjamin John, who died in infancy, Ferdinand Fullerton, Charles Henry Samuel, Frederick Alexander and Mary Augusta. Marianne died in 1789 and Henry Perkins then married her cousin, Jeanne Marie Bergier du Mont.

By his second marriage he had six more children: John Samuel Henry, Francis William, George Horace, George Edward Nicholas, John Finch and Augustine Charles. Both Francis William and George Edward Nicholas, settled in New South Wales, Australia and George Edward Nicholas married Blanche, daughter of Lt. Col. George Johnstone of the 102nd Regiment. This lady was Great-grandmother to Bert Weston who came to England in 1993 and opened West Horsley's Summer Fete.

During most of Henry Perkins life, West Horsley Place was let to tenants, first to a solicitor, Avery Tebb and then to Lord Farnham who was here in the late 1760s. It is not certain when Henry Perkins Weston returned to live at Horsley but he was a Justice of the Peace nine times between 1792 and 1821. His second wife died in 1804 and he died and was buried here in 1826.

The eldest son, Ferdinand Fullerton, succeeded to the estate, but died without a male heir in 1835. He had married Harriet Eliza Babington at St Mary's in 1808, but they only had one daughter, Anne Henrietta, so the estate passed to his younger brother, Charles Henry Samuel Weston, M.A. who had become an Anglican clergyman and since 1804 had been assisting the Rector, Weston Fullerton, as curate until he himself became Rector in 1816. When he inherited the estate in 1835 he was then both Rector and Lord of the Manor until he resigned his living in 1842.

The third brother, Frederick Alexander had become a Colonel in the service of the East India Company but died in 1837, so when his brother Charles, who had remained a bachelor all his life, died in 1849, the estate passed to the eldest son of Henry Perkins' second marriage, Colonel John Samuel Henry Weston, C.B.

Colonel John Weston also served in India, which is where his first wife died in 1826. She was Sarah MacGregor and bore him two children, Mary Isabella and Henry. Colonel Weston married twice more. By the second wife, Margaret Nicholson, he had three daughters and a son before she died in childbirth in 1838, then he married Jessie Playfair and had another son.

CRANMORE

Colonel John Weston died at Chilworth in 1850, aged 59, but was buried at West Horsley. He was succeeded by his eldest son, Henry, who, two years later, married a lady called Frances Harriet. They had four children, Frances, Henry MacGregor, Charles Edward and Walter John. Henry died in Middlesex when he was only 38 but was brought to West Horsley to be buried. His eldest son, Henry MacGregor Weston, inherited the estate in 1863 when Henry Currie the banker was in residence at The Place. He had a new plain Victorian house built for himself to live in which he called Cranmore after the pond that used to lie behind it. It is now Cranmore School.

When Henry Currie died in 1873, West Horsley Place was let to Mr and Mrs George Fielder and it was not until Mrs Fielder died in 1908 that Henry MacGregor Weston went to spend the last eleven years of his life in the house. He died in 1919 and his nephew, Major Charles Francis Russell Nugent

This picture was taken in about 1905 by Harry Robinson who had the Post Office in the village at this time and produced his own postcards. It shows the Surrey Union Hunt meeting outside West Horsley Place.

Weston, son of his brother Charles, inherited the estate. He lived there with his first wife, Dorothy Janet Agnes, who was a cousin and also a Weston, the daughter of an Indian Army Colonel. They had three children, two sons and a daughter, and remained living at West Horsley Place until after the First World War when the rising costs and taxes forced him to sell the estate in 1921 together with the famous Nicholas collection of portraits.

The Place was bought by Lady Cooper, and 10 years later it was sold to the Marquis and Marchioness of Crewe, whose daughter Mary, Duchess of Roxburghe, inherited it at her mother's death in 1967.

Although the West Horsley estate had been sold, the title of Lord of the Manor and the advowson of the church remained with the Weston family. They emigrated to New Zealand where Major Charles Weston died in 1951. The advowson passed to his second wife, Kitty, who returned to England with her son, Colonel A.R.N. Weston, who lives in Oxfordshire. He is the present Lord of the Manor and holds the advowson to St Mary's Church.

The Weston Family, Rectors 1758-1893

For well over a hundred years the Rectors of West Horsley were all related to the Weston family who were lords of the manor. In 1758 Henry Weston instituted his nephew, John Fullerton, B.C.L. who already held the living at Cobham, to the living at West Horsley. Then in the following year when his uncle died, John Fullerton became one of the guardians to his orphaned cousin, Henry Perkins Weston.

John Fullerton remained a batchelor while he was at West Horsley and was made an archdeacon, but after he resigned his living here he went to one at All Cannings, Devizes and subsequently married and had two children.

John Fullerton's brother, Weston Fullerton, L.L.B., had become his curate in 1762 and succeeded him as Rector in 1770. He was instituted by his cousin, Henry Perkins Weston who by this time had come of age. This Rector was also a batchelor. He was a wealthy man, and had the reputation for generosity and benevolence. However, in 1775, a curate called George Bray came to the parish and from then on, nearly all the services including baptisms, marriages and burials were conducted by the curate.

Shortly before he resigned his living in 1816 at the age of 81, Weston Fullerton endowed a little wooden schoolroom to be used as a Sunday School for poor children where they could learn elementary reading, writing and arithmetic as well as the scriptures. In those days poor children started work at about the age of six years and had little opportunity of receiving an education.

In 1804, Charles Weston, third son of Henry Perkins Weston by his first marriage, became curate and when Weston Fullerton resigned his living in 1816, his father instituted him as Rector. In contrast to many of his predeces-

The Parsonage House, West Horsley (from an old print)

sors, Charles Weston lived in West Horsley for most of his time and took nearly all the church services.

The main part of the old Parsonage House, as it had been called until that time, was probably built before 1400 like the old Tithe Barn which still stands behind it, but from the only drawing that remains of it, there were probably some Tudor and Jacobean additions. It was said to be in a dilapidated condition, so in order to make it his home, Charles Weston had the oldest part pulled down, and incorporating part of the east wing as well as the Jacobean addition at the back, he had the house rebuilt in the Regency style and was able to move into it in 1819. From 1821 he also held the living of Ockham.

In 1835 Charles Weston became both Rector and lord of the manor when his eldest brother died without a male heir. In the same year he appointed his nephew, Henry Sigismund Cerjat M.A. aged 25, as curate. He was the son of Charles Weston's sister, Mary Augusta, who had married a Swiss, Charles Sigismund Cerjat.

In 1840, when Henry Currie the banker was resident at West Horsley Place, he advanced £200 for rebuilding Church Cottage and its outbuildings in East Lane to replace an older cottage which stood there and belonged to the church. This was for the curate to live in and the money was to be paid back by the church at £16 a year.

61

Charles Weston resigned in 1842, seven years before his death and Henry Sigismund Cerjat was instituted as Rector of St Mary's in the same year. He did not marry until 1846 when he was 33. His bride was Frances Charlotte Perceval, the young daughter of the Rector of East Horsley, but sadly she died after only a few months of marriage at the age of 19.

After his tragic loss, Henry Cerjat devoted himself to parish affairs and his sister Eliza Anne, also born in Lausanne like himself, kept house for him. It was another 16 years before he remarried, and this time it was to a lady from Yorkshire, called Esther Louisa Wynne. This was in 1862 and from 1879, we find that he had begun signing his name "de Cerjat".

In 1845 the little Sunday school had been endowed still further by Charles Weston, but Henry Cerjat decided the facilities were not adequate. There was a growing feeling in the 19th century, especially among religious bodies, that all children should have at least the chance of some kind of elementary education. So in 1861 he built St Mary's School with his own money on some land he had purchased. A year after the school was opened he conveyed the ownership of it to the Bishop of Winchester in whose diocese West Horsley then lay. He directed that the school should be "for the education of children and adults, or children only, of the labouring, manufacturing and other poorer classes" and should be run "according to the Principles of the Church of England".

His school consisted of the two main classrooms of the present building, but at that time it was one big room with a gallery. Charles Weston's endowment to his predecessor's little schoolroom was transferred to the new school. In 1862 Henry Cerjat gave the orchard to the school, the rent from which was to provide a further endowment. In 1867 he built the school mistress's house onto the end of The Old Schoolhouse, which in those days was three cottages belonging to the church. The central cottage had at one time been used as a Dame School.

In the same year he built the village reading room, which later became used by the school as an extra classroom and the school kitchen and lunch room. Village Reading Rooms were built in most villages in those days so that the labouring classes could have an alternative place to go to from the alehouses. There would be newspapers and journals for them to read which they could not afford to buy for themselves, and tea and soft drinks were provided. In 1871 he also built the houses at the bottom of School Lane, one of which was for the school caretaker, and in 1892 he added the infant's room onto the school.

Henry de Cerjat died in 1893, aged 80 and was buried beside his first wife among the Weston graves. He had served the parish for a total of fifty-five years, first as a curate and then as Rector. In their tribute to him the Church Vestry wrote – "during this long period this parish received at his hands many and lasting benefits".

For 135 years the Rectors of West Horsley had been members of the Weston family; the chain was now broken when Stephen Hill, M.A. was instituted as Rector. He had been curate here for nine years, but he was only Rector for two years. In 1895 Edward Carl Unmack, D.D. was instituted by Henry MacGregor Weston and remained in office until 1934.

St Mary's School, built in 1861, with the infant's room on the right which was added in 1892.

The flint part of this building on the right was built in 1867 as the Village Reading Room. The brick addition on the left was probably built in the same year as the infant's room.

12

St. Mary's Church
Since The Reformation

After the Reformation when Rood Lofts with their minstrel galleries were taken down, there came a need to provide new locations for the church musicians, and galleries at the west end of the nave became popular to meet this need. The church orchestra would have consisted of woodwind, string and brass, and the musicians would have been all local villagers.

St Mary's west gallery was probably erected early in the 17th century. It was constructed of wood supported on four wooden posts and stretched between the east and west nave walls and the tower wall. A dormer window was inserted on the south side of the Nave roof to light it, and for access to the gallery, a small arched doorway was cut into the tower wall at first floor level. This was when the tower had two rooms in it, one above the other, which were reached by climbing the old Norman ladder. The first floor in the tower has since been removed.

Before the Reformation St Mary's tower had four bells in it, and the ancient bell-frame still has spaces for them, but the original ones probably disappeared at the time of the Reformation. The three bells that we have now all have dates inscribed on them. The 10 cwt (508 kg) bell is dated 1621, which was during the period when the second Viscount Montague held the manor. It was made by Bryan Eldridge of Chertsey, as was the second bell weighing 5 cwt (254 kg), which bears the date 1645 when Carew Raleigh held the manor. The third bell, weighing 7 cwt (355 kg) is dated 1687 and was probably a gift from John Nicholas when he held the manor. It was made by William Eldridge, the last of the family of bell-founders.

The bell-ringers must have rung the bells from the first floor of the tower because, it was said, they held meetings in the tower room and drank ale there when they practised their 'changes', for until 1786 the bells rang out with rounds and changes. There was a great deal of wear and tear on the ropes which meant that a new set of ropes and leather thongs for the clappers had to be bought every year. The bell frame and wheels were repaired in 1780, and by 1787 the fourth bell (date unknown) had cracked, so only three bell-ropes were renewed.

An inventory of 1553, included "3 chalices double gilte" and a note was added saying that since the inventory of 1549, there were several other items which had been "lost" (either stolen, taken away by the Church Commissioners, or simply hidden away). The present Church Plate, now deposited in the V. & A. Museum for safety, consists of a small silver cup and paten hall-marked 1634 at the time when Sir Anthony Browne was here, and another larger paten and a silver flagon, both hall-marked 1666 which were gifts from Sir Edward Nicholas. Sir Anthony Browne was a Roman Catholic, and he may have given the church the smaller paten and cup from the private chapel at West Horsley Place when he sold Horsley House.

The chapel at West Horsley Place was later converted into a sitting room by one of the Nicholas family, and according to an old family retainer, when the flagstones were being taken up, an earthenware pot was discovered which was thought to contain human viscera. There is no record of who they could have belonged to, perhaps to Sir Walter Raleigh or maybe one of the previous owners of the manor who had been beheaded or embalmed.

In 1810, the antiquarians, Manning and Bray paid a visit and described both church and tower as having flint covered walls on the exterior. They also said that the roof was tiled except for that of the north aisle which still retained the old Horsham slab slates which had once covered the whole roof.

Also in 1810, the Rev. Weston Fullerton carried out extensive repairs to the church costing about £3,000. The interior roof timbers were strengthened and enclosed by a plastered wagon ceiling in the nave and south aisle. The scar left by this ceiling can be seen on the east wall of the nave. The brick floor was replaced by York flagstones and it was at this time that the panel from the medieval alabaster reredos, smashed at the time of the Reformation, was found in the corner under the present pulpit.

A new three-decker pulpit made of pine was donated and inserted into the south-west corner of the nave, covering half of the chancel screen, and new chest-high box pews, each with its own door, were placed in the nave and south aisle.

It is not known where the original vestry room was, unless this was also in the tower. However, at this time, a new vestry room was built between the east end of the north aisle and the north wall of the chancel which blocked most of the de Berners window. There was an arched doorway into it from the aisle and a triple-light flat-topped window on the east wall. There was a fireplace and an unsightly chimney-stack on the north-east corner.

A watercolour by J. Hassel of the exterior west view of the church dated

West Horsley Church in about 1800. This is a picture of the north-east side from a drawing in the Minet Library, Camberwell. It shows the earlier north aisle and Jacobean porch.

1823 shows the shingled spire surmounted by a ball and vane and a thick growth of ivy on the tower. The narrow north aisle had no west window and a path ran from the church gate in the direction of Church House where there was a stable for the Rector's horse and an earth closet.

In the same year when Cracklow did his drawing from the south side of the church, he said that the church walls which were built of flint and mortar and lined with chalk had been plastered over, and he mentioned the west gallery and the new vestry room. It is a great pity that plaster was put over the flint walls, because we could have learned quite a lot from the old flint. It is quite possible in this more enlightened age to deduce which is Saxon flintwork, which is Medieval flintwork, and also, of course, Victorian flintwork. We could also have seen scars left from former doors, windows, different roof levels and also when a wall had been altered.

There are more watercolours by J. Hassel dated 1827 which show details of the inside of the church. They depict the three-decker pulpit, the box pews, the Weston pew where the children's corner is now, the wagon ceiling and the arched door in the north aisle into the new vestry. The pictures also show us that there was wooden panelling all around the east end of the chancel reaching up to the window ledges and that a huge ornamental board upon

66

St Mary's Church interior in 1827, from a watercolour by E. Hassell

which were painted the Ten Commandments, the Creed and the Lord's Prayer covered the lower part of the three lancet windows on the east wall of the chancel.

In 1849 more major restoration work took place under the guidance of the architect Henry Woodyer of Guildford. The late Norman north aisle was pulled down and rebuilt to widen it by four feet, and new pine pews were placed in it. The new north aisle was given a much higher pitched roof covered with clay tiles instead of the lower pitched roof which had been covered with Horsham slab. Also the "new" vestry and the brick and timber Jacobean porch were demolished. The late Norman doorway was preserved and re-erected as the new doorway and the present porch with its seating ledges and double oak gates was built. The present oak door is a replica of the original one.

In the chancel the roof timbers were renewed, the wainscotting, old Decalogue boards and old Communion rails were removed and replaced with new ones. The Communion table was raised upon another step and a relief design of stone arches was built against the east wall below the window. Inside these arches were painted, in gold, dark blue and red, the Decalogue, Creed and Lord's Prayer with a cross in the central arch. The west gallery was demolished and the choir was now sometimes accommodated in front of the chancel screen and another row of plain benches was added for other occasions in front of the beautiful late-Medieval benches which have finely carved "poppy-heads" in a fleur-de-lys shape on the tops and elbows of the bench ends.

A new vestry room was built in the south-east angle between the chancel and the chapel. This had an outer door as well as an inner door and a fireplace and chimney was built in it as well as a bench running all round three sides of the room, presumably so that Church Vestry meetings could take place here. It was at this time that the drainage channel was dug around the outside of the church walls and a new stove was bought for heating the church. The medieval west porch was used as a coal bunker! The cost of all these alterations was born by the Rev. Charles Weston and his successor, the Rev. Henry Cerjat.

A watercolour dated 1867 shows us that by this time the old west window and the easternmost window in the south aisle had both been replaced. There are stained glass windows in the chapel and south aisle in memory of members of the Weston family and also Henry Currie who had been a tenant at West Horsley Place. The new rose window in the north aisle was placed there in memory of the Rev. Charles Weston.

By 1871, three-decker pulpits were no longer popular, so in St Mary's the top of the pulpit was sawn off and lowered to its present position. In 1887 the box pews were removed, with the exception of a few in the south aisle, and were replaced with the present ones. In 1892 a harmonium was placed beneath the easternmost arch of the north arcade.

The 20th Century

St Mary's Church is the oldest building in this parish and in consequence the stones and mortar and ancient timbers need repairing, conserving or renewing at frequent intervals. The whole history of our parish was once mirrored in this lovely old building, for if we think about it, every item lost is a page torn from the book of the church's history, and indeed, the history of this parish.

Who had the alabaster reredos made and what did it look like when it was complete? Who gave the stained glass? Who had the chantry chapel built and why? Who gave the church silver? These are some of the questions I have tried to answer. More difficult to ascertain was, for example, how much was lost at the time of the Reformation. Was this a fairly simple country church or was the wealth of the parish reflected in the richness of the church furnishings? And were any of the people buried under the floor wool merchants or clothiers? And how many memorials to the families at the Manor House have we lost?

During the Reformation the church was stripped of many decorative objects from the Medieval period which enhanced its beauty, and in recent times, much has been lost to us through theft. However, although most of the stained glass windows were smashed, we still have some good examples of ancient glass. In 1909 the two Medieval glass medallions were removed from the side lancets in the chancel and placed in the lancets above the altar and a new one depicting the Annunciation was inserted in the third lancet to balance them.

In 1912 the first restoration work of the century took place. The spire was strengthened with new timbers and the old ceramic tiled floor in the chancel was taken up and replaced with stone flags. The nave roof was stripped and repaired and the pews and other woodwork which had formerly been a light colour, were stained dark brown. The medieval west porch was repaired, and the floor of the Nicholas chapel, which had suffered subsidence causing the monuments against the walls to come away, was strengthened and the monuments were cleaned and made safe.

While this work was being carried out, three discoveries were made:

Firstly a third lancet window was uncovered in the north wall of the chancel which had been blocked and hidden at some time in the past. Secondly, when repairing the east wall of the nave, the remaining half of an arched doorway was discovered which contained a step. Some thought this was the bottom of a staircase, but it was more likely to have been a step up into the chancel. Above this half arch there is a crude wooden door frame, which may have been to do with the rood loft. There would most likely have been a wooden staircase or ladder on the chancel side of the loft, and as the present north wall of the chancel abuts directly behind these two openings it proves that at some time since the Reformation, the north wall of the chancel must have been moved inwards to try and centralize a newly enlarged chancel arch. This bears out my theory that the original Saxon chancel must have been the same width as the nave and that there may have been three small arches, before two of them were made into one larger one. [See page 8.]

The third discovery was made by a choir boy who had been given the

task of scrubbing the dirty walls – it was part of the medieval wall paintings on the west wall of the nave. The extent of these were not realised until 1972 when the limewash was carefully uncovered and the paintings restored.

In 1921 Major Weston presented a brass candelabrum for six candles to hang in the nave. It was similar to the Jacobean one that was already hanging there. Unfortunately both of these were stolen in

69

recent years. In 1934, the Rector at the time, the Rev H. Stevens, gave a brass cross and candlesticks for the main altar, which had been made for him when he was a naval chaplain on H.M.S. Iron Duke. Another gift he made to St Mary's was a 16th century Greek tryptich, portraying the Virgin and Child, which he had acquired when he was a naval chaplain in Malta. Both this and the brass candlesticks were stolen.

Perhaps the most important event in the affairs of our parish church took place in 1927 when the diocese of Guildford was formed and our church was transferred from the diocese of Winchester to that of Guildford.

In the 1930s a group of ladies under Miss Dora Roscoe, a cousin of Beatrix Potter, made a number of embroidered articles for the sanctuary including two altar frontals and some kneelers. Miss Roscoe made the altar rail kneelers herself. Now we have another group of people, both ladies and gentlemen, making kneelers and also vestments for the Rector.

In 1934 a small electricity transformer was placed against the north church-yard wall and electric lighting was installed at 24 points in the church. Until that date the church had been lit by 22 oil lamps.

In the following year the wagon ceiling was removed from the nave and south aisle in case of beetle infestation in the roof timbers, and several years later the tower had to be fumigated because of an attack of beetle and other insects. These in turn had caused an attack by woodpeckers which were making large holes in the spire shingles!

In 1939, when the second world war started, the church had to have black-out curtains at each window and the de Berners tomb was covered with sandbags. The precious ancient glass was removed from the windows and stored until the end of the war. In 1940 a credence table was given by an anonymous donor for the sanctuary. It was said to have come from the Manor House at Rochdale, once the home of Lord Byron. That, too, has been stolen recently.

In 1945 it was decided to obtain a second-hand organ to replace the decrepit harmonium. One was eventually found for sale at Crookham Barracks for the sum of £800. Being over-large for our church, the only place it could be put was in the Nicholas Chapel, which was unfortunate, for it completely filled the once-beautiful chapel and hid from view the stained-glass window and the marble monuments.

In 1949 negotiations began for acquiring some land in East Lane on which to build a new church hall or Daughter Church. On this, in 1954, a new Rectory was built as the Old Rectory was too large to manage without servants. Then finally, in 1963 the new Daughter Church was built.

In 1953 the Weston pew was converted into a Children's Corner, the pulpit was stripped of its dark paint and a wall safe was fitted beside the north door. This has also been stolen.

In 1970 again more restoration work was carried out, this time costing around £5,000. It was at this time that the medieval wall paintings were restored with the help of a grant from the Central Council for the Care of Churches.

In 1974 the contents of the stone coffin in the wall beside the altar were examined with the aid of an endoprobe with a fibre-light guide inserted through a small hole. It was found to be filled with rubble. Originally this coffin would have been free standing and probably had a Latin inscription upon it. As I suggested, it might have contained the remains of the 2nd Sir Hugh de Windsor who rebuilt the chancel in 1210 AD. It is possible that when the north chancel wall was brought inwards a few feet at some time after the Reformation, it was built over the coffin, which was then filled with rubble to reinforce the lid. The de Berners tomb might also have been originally free standing and the wall was brought up against it. Outside you will see that the wall behind it protrudes slightly.

It is possible that the de Berners window was not in its present position; it may even have been in the south wall opposite to give more light in the chancel before the chapel was built and moved here later. In the Cracklow drawing of the church (page 29), there is a large window at the west end of the south aisle, now replaced, which looked like a chancel window. Could this have been the original chancel window which was replaced by three lancets when the chancel was made narrower?

This is the screen hiding the Nicholas chapel. The new pipe organ will be placed here and the chapel can then be restored. *[Photograph by Alan Bowley]*

There is no known record of this wall being moved inwards, but it was obviously done after the rood loft was removed and the chancel arch was enlarged, and certainly before 1800 when the earliest picture of this side of the church was drawn. (See page 66.)

Two innovations which have brought our church up-to-date are a sound enhancement system with an induction loop for hearing aids, and the installation of a telephone in case of emergencies.

Because the Victorian church organ is feeling its age and is rapidly falling apart, an appeal has been made to raise funds to buy a brand new church organ especially built for us. After much research by an expert committee, it was decided to buy a Frobenius two manual pipe organ, and an appeal was launched this year to raise its capital cost.

Christians have been worshipping on this site since at least the 9th century, about two hundred years before the foundations of this present church were laid. Let us hope that it will continue to be a centre for Christian worship for many centuries to come.

SOURCES

Guildford Muniment Room
Surrey Archaeological Society Library
Minet Library, Camberwell
Shirley Aston's "History of West Horsley"
Major Spencer's "Short History of West Horsley"
"Henry VIII and his Court" by Neville Williams

St. Mary's Church

This lovely church in ancient witness stands
Upon its lonely knoll, beside the way;
Some Saxon serf here knelt and cupp'd his hands,
A Norman noble too, in Knight's array,
Here came the villein with his wife and child,
The patron from the manor and his kin;
And through the years their sons and daughters filed,
Through Hist'ry's drama, peace or warfare's din.

Sir Hugh de Windsor, Richard Pykenot,
Sir Ralph de Berners, Widow Lee, John Stint;
And all the hamlet's children made their plot,
Each built his dwelling here in wood or flint,
And made forgotten conquests, played forgotten games.
They tilled the land, they built with brick and hod
And though we now forget their deeds and names
This church recalls their life, their love, their God.

Who painted frescoed Saints upon these walls?
Who built this aisle, or tolled the mattin bell?
Through Life's uncertain casting, hear their calls,
Their shrine lives here, the stones, the art retell;
In some small detail all the years unfold,
Through plague and peace and broken heart.
And now we share these grateful gifts of old,
And humbly pray we play our puny part.

John Stewart

73

St. Mary's Church, West Horsley.

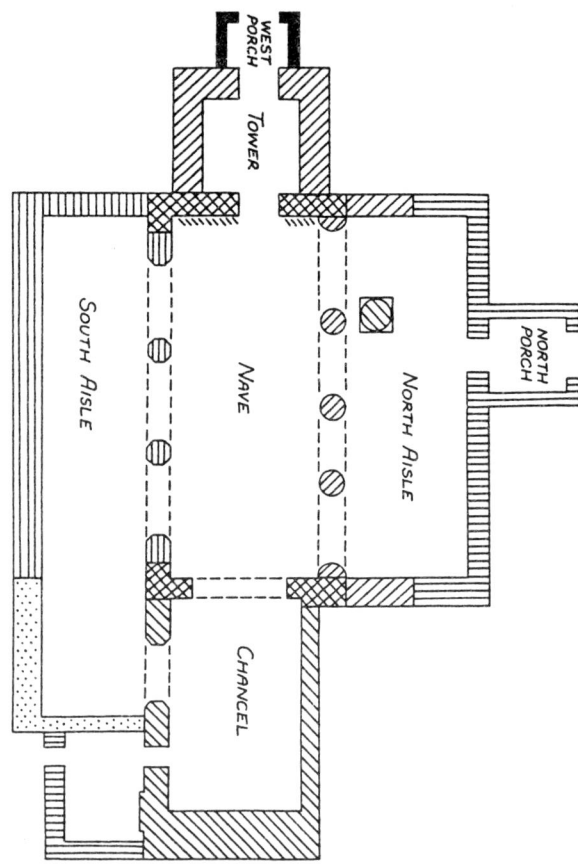

The Structural Evolution of St. Mary's Church, West Horsley

CENTURIES

- 11TH
- 12TH
- 13TH
- 14TH
- 15TH
- 16TH
- 19TH

WEST PORCH

TOWER

SOUTH AISLE

NAVE

NORTH AISLE

NORTH PORCH

CHANCEL

N
W—E
S

DRAWN TO SCALE 1-200

74